Lateral Work
Training for a supple horse

Lateral Work
Training for a supple horse

by Johannes Beck-Broichsitter

CADMOS

Dedicated to my father,
for whom I have more to thank than I ever realised.

Copyright © 2009 by Cadmos Verlag GmbH, Schwarzenbek
Copyright of this edition © 2009 by Cadmos Books, Great Britain
Design and setting: Ravenstein + Partner, Verden
Cover Photo: Christiane Slawik
Photography: Christiane Slawik
Drawings: Cadmos Archive, Philippe Karl, Maria Mähler
Editor: Anneke Bosse (original edition),
Linda Robinson, Christopher Long (this edition)
Translation: Claire Williams
Print: Westermann Druck, Zwickau

British Library Cataloguing in Publication Data
A catalogue record of this book is available from the British Library.
Printed in Germany

ISBN 978-3-86127-973-0

www.cadmos.co.uk

Contents

Foreword

Johannes Beck-Broichsitter has been influenced by renowned equestrians, who have successfully focused on classical riding and have often set new trends in training theories. Thanks to this background he has gathered experience in a variety of riding styles and training methods. In classical riding, depending on a number of secondary factors, a variety of methods can have the same outcome.

They are not exclusive of each other, but rather can complement one another. What is, for one method of training and riding, of primary importance will be more intensively worked on. What is considered less important may be neglected. For another approach to riding however this same factor may have priority with a great deal of attention paid to it. If a horse's suppleness is a central theme in training for classical dressage, then for western riding it is calmness even under exceptional external influences.

Representatives of both riding styles can, with regards to classical principles, learn from each other.

Johannes Beck-Broichsitter takes these different perspectives into consideration when teaching, in order to broaden his two-legged pupils' horizons for the benefit of their four-legged partners. This book, highlighting so many aspects on the theme of lateral movements, is an expression of the author's fundamental approach, which is to test the insights of others without any prejudice as to their applicability. It thus makes a tremendous contribution towards a growing tolerance within the riding world. Human vanity in this sphere leads directly towards frequent and unnecessary differences of opinion amongst experts. One can't help but be reminded of the observation that "Every peacock has the most beautiful feathers". Through a wide distribution of this book one hopes that Johannes Beck-Broichsitter will succeed in harmonising differing experts' opinions.

Richard Hinrichs
Wedemark, January 2009

Introduction

"Approaching Lateral Movements" was the working title of this book, since it seemed to best describe what I was trying to achieve with the book: breaking down any possible obstacles and demonstrating a practical approach to lateral movements as an essential element in the gymnastic training of every ridden horse. At the forefront of this is, without doubt, the question "When out hacking, am I able to ride my horse from point A to B and get there at the time I wish whenever I want to?" That is the point, in fact more so the purpose, that I give to the training of a horse.

The lateral movements are able to support me in reaching this goal like no other riding exercise or movement. They underpin every phase of training – whether it be with the introduction of the first sidewards, suppling movements, the preparation and perfection of various training exercises or in the improvement of advanced lessons through interaction with other exercises. This book covers all of these areas.

I am aware that the subject of lateral movements is too broad to allow me to exhaustively cover every aspect. Therefore I have been guided by three principles whilst writing:

1. Making the initiation into lateral work as clear as possible for my pupils and avoiding them becoming scared of these – in other words creating a desire to learn more after the first attempt.

2. Creating, for the more advanced rider who is working towards more difficult work, the experience of working in-hand and out of this gaining the means to develop their own ideas.

3. Repeatedly highlighting the fact that lateral movements are not an end in themselves but rather a means to an end that must keep a link with reality. The execution of lateral movements can only ever be as good as they are helpful for the entire training – I will return to, what is for me, this central concept later.

Furthermore I would like to present to the many people who ride by themselves – as a helping hand – not only the prerequisites and the practical exercises for developing the lateral movements, but also provide for each of them a brief summary which should help them to feel what is the right way of riding these movements until they can have this checked at their next lesson.

A further chapter is taken up with the almost eternal question of weight distribution for the shoulder-in. Here I have looked both at the extensive literature on the subject and researched modern riding masters.

One thing remains to be said: there is no doubt that the fitness of all those involved as well as the equipment and the learning environments must have particular importance attached to them. These I take for granted and so will not give them especial attention.

I hope to be able to give every reader lots of ideas, and end my introduction with a wish, following a quote from Goethe: "Someone who brings a lot, will bring something for everyone and everyone will leave happy ... out of the manège."

The meaning and purpose of the lateral movements

Before I move on to the actual subject from a practical point of view, I would like to outline several additional thoughts that detail my approach when teaching, to make it easier for the reader to understand and follow the sense and purpose of the lateral movements from my point of view.

History

The co-existence of Man with horse has always been and is still today due to necessity over time. Over 6000 years of history, the relationship has been marked mainly by the fact that the horse has secured Man's survival – whether it be as a source of food or in war.

The relationship between horse and mankind was and is, of course, marked by other less threatening – for a horse's life – aspects, for example in his role as a means of transport, draught animal, fighting tool in jousting, work of art, object of prestige, pet, sports instrument, therapist or simply friend.

In the case of horses that in times past were trained for service in war, there was a difference between the training to be a driving as opposed to a riding horse. Regardless of the intended use, both needed to get to the field of war safely and without unnecessary loss of energy and then allow themselves be steered through the battle despite all the dangers.

He who owned a well trained horse that followed the commands of his rider, survived. The survival of a nation could depend on this. In this respect, it was necessary at an early stage to give thought to practical and appropriate training and breeding programmes.

I only have room to briefly cover the significant periods and important trainers of their time that provide relevant information on the theme of increasing suppleness through lateral work.

If you start your study in Greece then you will find yourself faced with Xenophon around 400 BC. As well as his essays on the psychology of the horse, on purchasing horses and on the training of young horses and young riders, his description on working on the circle is of particular use for us. Here the horse learns to "allow himself to be turned on both jaws". This refers to bending and flexing. Furthermore he demanded changing the rein through the circle or half circles interspersed with straight lines.

Here he was already talking of collection in the turns in order to improve balance. In addition – this will make western riders particularly pleased – he talks about the sense and purpose of sliding stops and short sprints or rollbacks to improve the flexibility of the forehand.

Fast-forwarding many centuries, we turn next to the Italian Frederico Grisone at the end of the sixteenth century. He counts as one of

At the end of the sixteenth century Georg Engelhard von Löhneysen described the riding of voltes together with the hind quarters bent to the inside of the circle – a form of travers. (Illustration: Cadmos Archive)

the leading Riding Masters of his time and is seen as the Father of Equitation since he was the first, after a gap of nearly 2000 years, to give systematic thought to the entire training of the horse.

Grisone recognised, amongst other things, the value of trot work to improve a horse's self carriage, the use of circles and uphill work to improve the use of a horse's hind quarters. He also mentions "positioning the horse through the withers", however being "soft, so that he doesn't become crooked through the neck".

A good 50 years later the German Riding Master Georg Engelhard von Löhneysen was already detailing the riding of voltes (small circles of 6 – 10 metres), whereby alternatively either the forehand or the quarters should be so positioned as to describe a smaller circle (i.e. as a sort of shoulder-in or travers).

Thanks to one of Grisone's pupils, these ideas and schooling exercises travelled to a number of locations, including France where in the seventeenth century Antoine de Pluvinel was at the court of Louis XIII. He was concerned particularly with in-hand work, since he felt that it "made the spirit contemplative and made the mind work more than the body". Furthermore he advocated a milder type of training – a subject that even then must have already been developing.

Exercises including the use of a pillar to work around and turns and movements sidewards under a rider with particular attention to the forwards movement are credited to him, because by using these, the horse stays "in his own rhythm and with good posture". Here one can see the origin for what we now consider to be the lateral movements. It must be said however that

Antoine de Pluvinel, already known in the seventeenth century for mild and humane training of horses, is here shown during instruction in front of King Louis XIII.

he rode in, simply put, a type of knight's saddle which, unlike for later generations of riders, did not allow a direct contact with the horse's sides. Any work involving bending or the movement of the quarters were achieved with a straight leg and spurs.

In England in the seventeenth century, William Cavendish, Duke of Newcastle, recommended the exercise "head to the inside on the circle", as well as the first indications of quarters in and out also on the circle. Also originating from him was the acknowledgment that a horse can only be collected when the hind legs are being placed on the ground closer together (moving on a narrow gauge).

The idea of a "sensitive leg that felt the horse's breathing and the hairs of his coat", originating from the German head groom Pinter von der Aue, also comes from this period. He also started to think about using a saddle that allowed the rider to bend his knee. However the idea for his saddle was really only implemented some 70 years later.

As you can see, even then grooms didn't have an easy life…

La Guérinière's "balance saddle" made it possible for the first time to really ride a horse up in to an outline using all the aids.

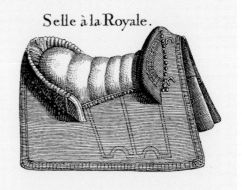

The meaning and purpose of the lateral movements

l'Épaule en Dedans.

14

The "inventor" of the shoulder-in:
François Robichon de la Guérinière with one of his
pupils. (Illustration: Cadmos Archive)

tracks. His teachings are still seen today by all those who practise classical equitation as the absolute foundation for their art. It is only surprising that he of all people never wrote about the distribution of weight in the shoulder-in – a question that is still debated with relish today. (See also from page 105.)

If riding in the Baroque period was, especially in France, still considered an art form in royal court life, then the French revolution proved to be a serious turning point, after which the art of equestrianism would have been almost forgotten had it not been, for example, for the Spanish Riding School in Vienna, which had adopted La Guérinière's teachings at an early stage. Many of the leading trainers of those, and indeed today's times, took and still take the opportunity to learn from the School's trained and accomplished riders. Thus a part of European culture that has matured over time still exists and is protected today.

The so-called "balance saddle" was eventually introduced on to the market by François Robichon de la Guérinière at the beginning of the eighteenth century. At last it became possible to school a horse completely with all the available aids.

Whether it was also he who "invented" the shoulder-in cannot categorically be determined today, especially since there were instructors before him who had spoken about exercises that sound very much like the first lateral movements. La Guérinière is however the first who had the shoulder-in ridden on a straight line. He gathered all of the essential parts from those who had gone before him and combined them to produce for us the mother of all other lateral movements – albeit on four

A brief definition

Lateral movements are defined as exercises in which the horse is flexed and bent. The horse will move on three or four tracks in a constant forwards – sideways direction in collection. We differentiate between shoulder-in, travers, renvers and half pass. The latter can also be differentiated, depending on the angle and other variables.

In addition one must also include the "counter" or "opposite" versions, although the shoulder-in is the only one where there is really a "true" counter version, since a counter travers is the same as renvers and vice versa. Although not lateral movements in the true sense of the words, but belonging to the same

The lateral movements at a glance.

Shoulder-in.

Travers or renvers on the centre line, depending on where it is positioned.

Counter shoulder-in.

Half pass.

The similarity of the lateral movements

RENVERS
on the right rein

TRAVERS
on the left rein

COUNTER SHOULDER-IN
on the right rein

SHOULDER-IN
on the left rein

TRAVERS
on the right rein

RENVERS
on the left rein

SHOULDER-IN
on the right rein

COUNTER SHOULDER-IN
on the left rein

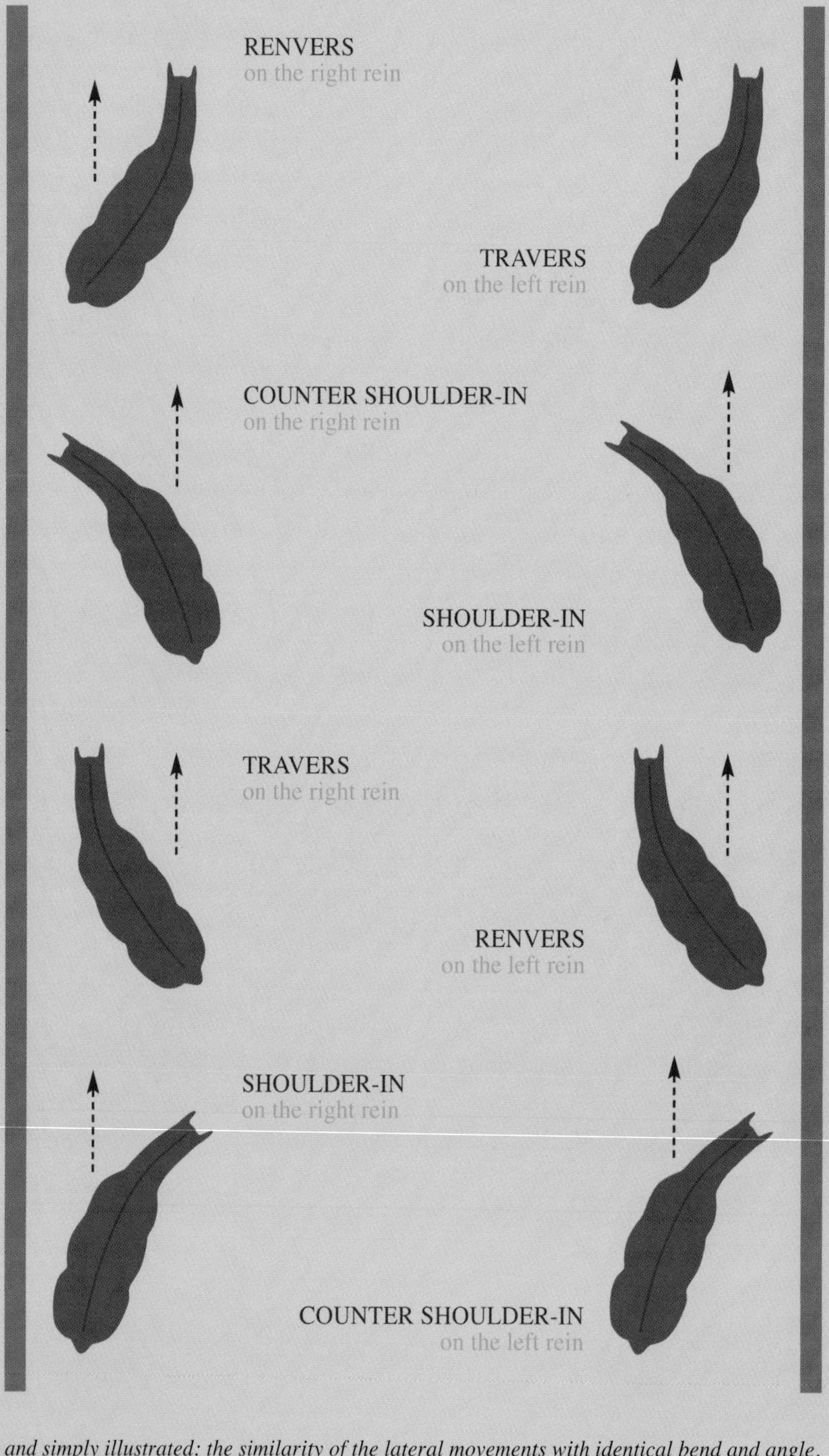

Clearly and simply illustrated: the similarity of the lateral movements with identical bend and angle.

The result of dressage training should not only be the ability to hack out safely. Conversely, it should be possible to "do" dressage when out riding.

family of movements, shoulder fore and riding in position to the inside or outside should also be considered. They are often referred to as "semi shoulder-in" or "half travers" since they give both horse and rider the first indication of what will be coming in the lateral movements to follow.

"Trot flexion" for shoulder fore and "canter flexion" for riding in position are also terms that are less often used today. The terms originate from the fact that – simply put – the trot flexion improves the trot, but makes it more difficult for the horse to transition into canter, whilst the canter flexion encourages precisely that.

Nowadays in competition the lateral movements are only asked for at medium level, once collection has been established, whilst shoulder-in, for example, is required until Intermediaire 1.

Dressage riders are relieved of having to do travers and renvers part way through medium level. From here the emphasis is on the half pass. In the case of eventing, however, riders in two star competitions must show travers and shoulder-in and in three and four star classes both shoulder-in and half pass are required.

"Lateral movements are always being ridden incorrectly. Irregular crossing over of the legs, irregular steps, no bend or flexion, false bend and so on. Often we see loss of rhythm and impulsion during lateral movements. Lateral movements are the measure of a well ridden horse."

Egbert Röschmann, international dressage judge

Why lateral movements?

The good thing about lateral movements is that they are not ridden as an end in themselves but instead offer everyone great possibilities to develop themselves and their horses further.

Even the first attempts offer a variety of possibilities for improving suppleness that at the same time reflect your own efforts.

The merits of lateral work for the horse:

- Helps in straightening.
- Strengthening the musculature, especially improving the flexibility and the carrying power of the hind quarters.
- Improvement of balance and, with this, the freeing up of the shoulders.
- Improvement of suppleness and attentiveness.
- Encourages mental composure and longer concentration.
- Trains the horse's awareness of his own body.
- Encourages forwardness and the desire to move forward.
- Trains obedience to the aids.
- Helps to improve suppleness and submissiveness into old age.
- Exercises that, once practised, will be recognised again in the future and that can be called on at a later date.

- Overcoming any difficulties through targeted work.
- Relaxes the horse (at advanced stages of training).

Merits for the rider:
- Effectively corrects natural crookedness.
- Being taught to use the aids effectively.
- Learning the targeted use of the seat aids.
- Awareness of the use of lateral work in everyday training.
- Training the diagonal aids and "framing" of the horse.
- Development of problem solving solutions through the targeted use of lateral movements.
- Learning to be satisfied with less.

Merits for the trainer:
- Learning how to analyse a sequence of movements.
- Recognising the individual strengths and weaknesses of horse and rider.
- Composing a lesson plan that demands more mental than physical effort.
- Development of a customised lesson plan for every rider-horse partnership.
- Awakening in the pupil a sense of the different ways to solve problems in training.
- Encouraging the desire to learn more.

Prerequisites
for horse and rider

It is well known that everyone, whether horse or human, is born crooked or one-sided. If however two one-sided beings meet and want to achieve something, then complications can easily arise. The following chapter should therefore be a mental foundation stone for the most effective way to proceed.

Natural crookedness and initial attempts at straightening

Every horse is by nature crooked; in other words he has an inborn lopsidedness of the spine. This is comparable with people being right or left handed and is made worse by the fact that his forehand is narrower than his quarters. This means that an unbacked horse will never look as straight and his hind legs will not stand in line with his front legs, i.e. be on the same track.

This crookedness is in this respect a natural necessity so that the long-legged foal doesn't catch his front legs with his back legs in canter or gallop.

For the sake of convenience we will look further into the case where a horse is crooked (or hollow) to the right, whereby the muscles on the right hand side are shorter than the left and allow the right hind leg to move past the centre of gravity and avoid the need to bend. He will step to the side and right next to the

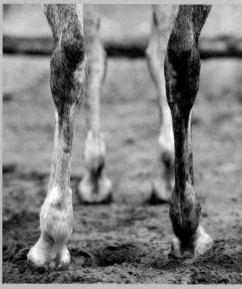

The crooked horse: the quarters are by nature wider than the forehand.

One goal of training is therefore to straighten the horse so that the forehand and hind quarters step over one another.

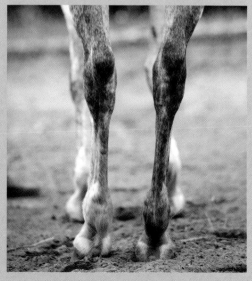

21

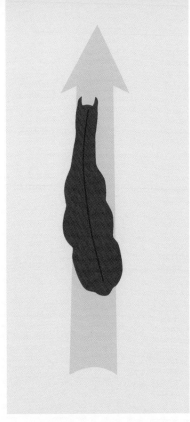

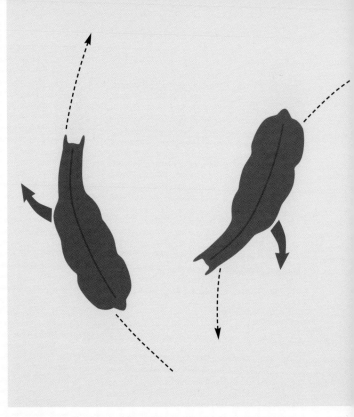

22

The effect of natural crookedness:
The horse that hollows to the right
pushes off from the right hind to the
front left and puts more strain on the
left hand side.

He will tend to fall out through the left shoulder when turning or
bending to the right, making the turn larger, whilst when turning
to the left he will fall on to the left shoulder and make a smaller
turn or circle.

track of the right fore. In this position the right hind will develop more thrust whilst the left will have less room to move and must bend more. In addition the left fore leg must absorb the increased amount of thrust and will put more strain on the left shoulder.

For the rider, a horse that is crooked to the right will give the following feeling:

- He will sit more to the right.
- The horse will appear to step through to the left rein more easily.
- The left shoulder is harder to move since this side is overloaded.
- On the right rein the right hind leg will edge into the school off the track.
- On the right rein the horse will be harder to move away from the edge of the school, will

be harder to ride on the inside track, always trying to get back out to the outside track.
- On the left rein the horse will always tend to the inside with the right hind leg sticking to the outside track.
- In the case of unclear aids or aids that are too strong, especially where the hand is too strong, the horse will have problems maintaining his outlines, either curling up, tilting the head, over bending or similar.

For the rider to continue schooling a horse in this condition without trying to straighten him, can be compared to a weightlifter continuously lifting 30 kg with his right arm and 50 kg with the left. The result is obvious: such unevenness can only lead to unnecessary and premature wear and tear.

Problems with the horse's rhythm or even bridle lameness are the most obvious results. In the wild this one-sidedness would make no difference to the horse. With a rider however, he suddenly has a weight on his back, which as a flight animal he is neither physically nor mentally equipped for.

The thinking rider, taking a systematic approach, is therefore challenged with:

- Helping the horse, when carrying the rider's weight on his back, to achieve mental and physical balance.
- Training the horse so that all muscles are worked evenly.

An important goal when training: horse and rider not only enjoy each other but are also in mental and physical balance.

- Controlling the right hind leg and teaching it to bend and follow in the same track as the right fore.
- Protecting and if possible relieving the left shoulder.
- Encouraging the left hind leg to take up an even share of providing the forward thrust.

This straightening work – which is a central theme throughout a horse's training – must also take into consideration a horse's fitness, age, ability to concentrate and most importantly his ability to go forwards; remember that every movement of the head and neck, every flexion or degree of bend as his training advances, can interfere with his forwards movement.

For this reason I keep this following quote from Richard Hinrichs constantly at the back of my mind:

23

"Only he who is in motion can be steered."

Richard Hinrichs

Against a background of starting this straightening work, I will initially take advantage of the horse's natural balance. This means that on the right hand I will give the horse the chance to be positioned and slightly bent to the left on turns. I am thus offering him the chance to take up a position that he would chose if running loose, in order to balance himself.

By doing this I am able, with very few aids, to take some of the weight off the left shoulder as well as also encourage the left hind to carry more weight and the right hind to track up in line with the fore. Once the horse becomes more balanced, then I can gradually ask for more and more inside bend and flexion.

On the lunge a young horse will balance himself to the outside.

On the left rein the challenge is to work against the horse's urge to fall in through the shoulder. One valuable exercise that I like to use is to ride as described above with left bend and flexion on the right rein and then change to the left rein without changing the bend. I will then, for a short time, have less strain on the shoulder to the inside. I now try to keep this on a large curved line. Also helpful is changing which leg you are rising on in trot, as you will then engage the inside hind more, as it lifts up and moves forward into the turn more energetically. Later this will help you ride different turns through to the initial stages of shoulder fore with less difficulty.

In using these exercises I am making the most of the following fact: after changing the rein the horse can better see where he is going and enjoys the relief it provides as well as being able to move straight ahead. The result is that the better I am able to influence the horse's movement simply through changing direction then the more likely I am to be able to influence the forehand through the reins and the quarters through my leg (supported by my weight). Thus the foundation for a horse's systematic education following the scales of training is laid.

Should I also be faced with conformational problems in addition to his natural crookedness, then I may need to turn off the more direct path and use plan B in order to return to the path more effectively later on.

Should I, for example, be faced with a horse that is too straight through his hocks then my attention will be focused on activating his quarters: working him in hand on large circles, lunging him to improve his overall suppleness and mobility with attention to increased bend and crossing over of his hind legs or even lunging over cavaletti to encourage more lifting and bending of his legs.

If you can refine this then in the ongoing work on straightening, with a view towards collection, whether it be in increased bend or the angle in your lateral movements or by shifting your work on to another line or through the inclusion of shoulder fore and shoulder-in, then we have the best possible exercises "for and against everything" at our disposal.

If I can use all the lateral movements then in many different ways I have been given a treasure trove of goodies to access that allows me to activate the forehand as well as the hind quarters. This will prevent premature wear and tear and will in the end lead to a regular strengthening of the muscles, improved balance, a more secure straightness, more sensitivity to the aids and increased "throughness" or suppleness (the German term for this, Durchlässigkeit, has no direct translation in English, but is a combination of this together with the submissiveness to the aids).

For horses with conformation faults, such as here where the angle through the hind legs is too straight, then plan B or even plan C is needed to help horse and rider.

The result of regular and systematic gymnastic work: good outline with an active hind leg.

A good outline: the neck vertebrae are lifting through the shoulders.

About the anatomy

26

The horse was not by nature intended to carry weight. Thus training must be used to turn an animal of flight into one suitable to be ridden. Lateral work is perfect for strengthening the horse's musculature for this purpose.

The purpose of schooling the horse must be to overcome his natural crookedness and inclination to overburden his forehand whilst bringing him back into a balance that allows him to carry himself and a rider's weight – even sometimes over jumps.

In order to try to give my pupils a clearer and more understandable way to reach this goal, I ask them to imagine a horse stretching over a fence to reach the grass that (of course) always tastes better on the other side, without however touching the fence itself. In this position it is guaranteed that the all important nuchal (neck) and supraspinous (back) liga-

ments are tensed, thus making the muscles through the back movable.

The central and turning point is the trapezius muscle just in front of the withers. Here the nuchal and supraspinous ligaments meet. But this is also where the muscles of the neck and back run together. When stretching forwards and downwards, the cervical vertebrae (those in the neck) lift up between the shoulders (scapula), stretching forwards, whilst at the same time the nuchal ligaments pull the spinous process of the vertebrae up, ensuring they are correctly aligned. This causes the back to rise and the muscles to stretch. This in turn allows the muscles running along the back to be released and relaxed, enabling the back to swing and be supple. This in turn will produce longitudinal suppleness as the back is raised and stretched, encouraging the stride to become longer and strengthening the back and quarters to allow for more engagement.

Definition of longitudinal bend

The term "longitudinal bend" is one that is much discussed amongst trainers. There is such a thing as longitudinal bend, however a constant or consistent bend through the entire body is not possible for anatomical reasons, since only the cervical and lumbar vertebrae are movable. The thoracic and sacral vertebrae have limited or no lateral movement.

When we talk about regularity of bend, we are talking more about the muscle action, the feeling of the rider or just an unawareness of a horse's anatomy which leads to this idea.

If the horse however is allowed to work behind the vertical or over bent then the muscles of the neck will be overworked and unsupported by the rest of the body. This creates the risk of the vertebrae in the neck dropping and making the horse heavy on the forehand.

Try it yourself when standing relaxed, letting your chin drop down onto your chest. Next draw yourself up and grow tall; now

A "true" longitudinal bend: here it is shown that for anatomical reasons the horse will always bend through the neck more than through the body, which almost stays straight even when moving laterally. (Drawing: Karl)

repeat the exercise with a long neck. You will be astonished, how much lowering your head extends through into your back!

Exactly the same applies to our horse.

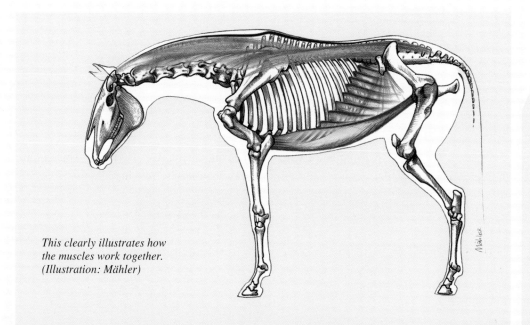

This clearly illustrates how the muscles work together. (Illustration: Mähler)

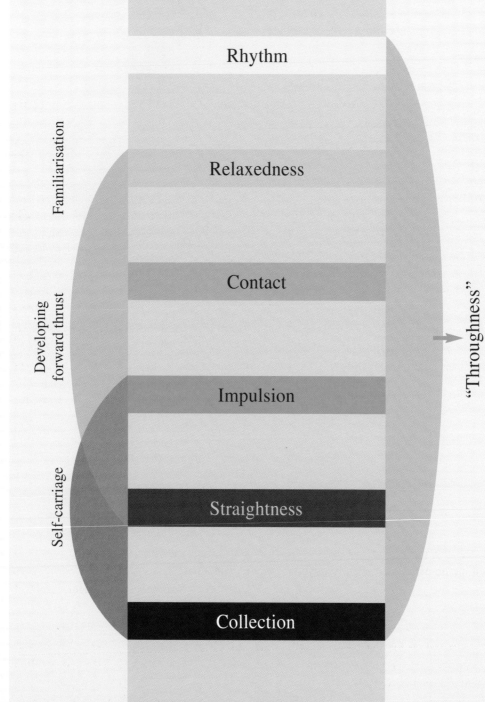

The Training Scale for Horses

Rhythm

Relaxedness

Contact

Impulsion

Straightness

Collection

Familiarisation

Developing forward thrust

Self-carriage

"Throughness"

Thoughts about the scale of training

Rather than an explanation of the already well known "Scale of training", I would like to restrict myself to the basic principles.

The Scale's beginnings were in the German service regulations from 1912 in the form of instructions for the training of young horses. In the first edition of the German Equestrian Federation's "Guidelines" issued in 1954, three phases of training are mentioned. In 1974, the following terms were used in this order: relaxation, strengthening of the muscles, regularity of the paces, contact, moving feely forwards, developing forward thrust and working from behind, straightness, beginnings of collection and then collection. In 1979, the Scale appeared for the first time in the form that we know it today – with the slight difference that rhythm and relaxation belonged to the first, familiarisation phase. This was only changed in 1994.

Although the order of the elements within the Scale are always being discussed, I will detail these in the order in which they are given in the Guidelines. If I didn't make this clear from the start, it would, not to put too fine a point on it, make the Scale a free for all, so that everyone would ride and train as they felt best.

More than this though the "official" order must become second nature to any rider. Only then will the rider when riding alone have something on hand to refer to. Remember – a clear structure gives a sense of security.

For this reason, when teaching, I also take the rider, to an extent, in hand and give direction until I can see that she is in a position to decide her own way in training. As soon as an overview and enough knowledge are available, my direct help moves into support.

"The Scale of training has developed and it will probably continue to do so."

*Thies Kaspareit,
the Equestrian Academy, 2008*

I will then discuss the pros and cons of the appropriate order with the pupil.

My approach can be compared with the help that I would give to a child who can't cross the road by itself. At some stage you have to let the child make his own way.

As a conclusion to this chapter I would like to offer some thoughts on the order and content of the Training scale itself. In the familiarisation phase, we are concerned, as the term suggests, with getting the horse used to the training process, introducing him not only to the saddle, bridle, his surroundings etc but also to the regularity of his movement (rhythm), his readiness, both internally and externally, to work through the relaxed tensing and relaxing of the musculature ("Losgelassenheit" in German, translated for our purposes as "relaxedness") and the constant connection with the rider's hand (contact).

It is important however to always keep in mind and be aware what the last two terms mean for the horse: he needs to physically and mentally let himself go – despite the unaccustomed weight of the rider. It must be remembered that only someone who is trusted and experiences a clear and regular contact, can in turn trust it himself.

In German the word used for contact is "Anlehnung", from the word meaning to lean or follow. Rather than a negative connotation, by it is meant that the horse should stretch out and follow where the hand leads. The horse

29

The goal of dressage training can be encompassed in a simple question:
Could I go for a canter when out hacking or must I worry that he is going to fall on his face due to a lack of
balance when he leaves the school?

can only do this when he can trust the hand and allow himself to be led. Think about dance partners, where the women puts her trust in her partner to lead her around the dance floor in the knowledge that he can see where they are going and will lead her with the right amount of contact. Or another picture is that of a couple in love who hold out their hands to help each other cross over a stream. What qualities must someone have for you to hold out your hand to them?

In the second phase of training, developing forward thrust, the power in the haunches will be channelled in the right direction. Building towards relaxedness and contact, using transitions and changes of tempo, the energy created in the quarters will be released forwards. In this way you are creating a steady frame which can be moved in every direction with the aim of improving his straightness.

In the development of self-carriage, the forwards impulsion that has been acquired will be transformed into an increased ability to carry more weight and more flexibility but also in an improved outline and a better, more secure balance. This is what we define as collection. For me this is connected with terms such as becoming more upright, growing, gaining confidence, seeing something from a different angle, having an overview, taking weight off the forehand and placing more weight through the haunches, being collected. All of these words typify what is involved in both the goals and the challenges contained in the entire training process: when, and most of all for how long, is a horse in a position to either lighten or take up more weight, never mind carry himself?

Frequently, far too much significance is placed on the engagement of the hind quarters, especially in the first two stages. So much so that the horse in the end is more active behind than his balance in front can cope with. The result is a constant strain, and riders who in effect are carrying their horses around the manège in the hope that through transitions or similar they will achieve lightness and the lifting of the forehand. What is frequently overlooked however is that once a horse is in the wrong position or his outline in the wrong carriage, then doing what has just been described will only cement the situation, not improve it, not to mention the wasted effort on both sides. If you are not fit then you will not have a chance. The first Chief Instructor of the Spanish Riding School in Vienna described this appropriately:

"If riding is as physically demanding, as many riders claim, then it can never become an art."

Arthur Kottas-Heldenberg

But it can be so easy. If I – to name but one example – am able at any time to ask the horse to stretch down to the contact, and afterward take up where I had left off, then I am heading in the right direction.

Thoughts about the aids

Every trainer not only has his own way of doing things and emphasises different aspects of training for both horse and rider, but also uses different, as I describe them, "user defined" vocabulary. So that you can better follow my thoughts in this book, I provide the following list of the terms that I like to use with my definitions. Occasionally I will use terms that seem to have nothing to do with riding, so without the background to them you could become confused.

• **Balance**
For me this is one of the main pillars of training. By this I mean not only physical balance but also most of all being mentally balanced. Only those who have an inner balance can become physically balanced. At the same time it is also a case of the more you are in physical balance, the greater the chance that you can be at peace with yourself.

• **Application of the aids**
The aids that are available to us are the only means we have of communicating with the horse about what we want from him. For this reason great importance is attached to their application.
The *leg aids* are all too often applied with too little discrimination. For many exercises the leg is always immediately further back: to halt and to move off, for the rein back, leg yielding, for riding circles and to canter. How is a horse supposed to know what you want – unless the joint application of the other aids play a role of course?
In the case of the *rein aids*, similar reasoning applies. It is human nature to carry out the majority of our jobs with the hands. Add to this your head, that sometimes finds it difficult to let things out of your hands; in other words, it just doesn't trust enough to let go. If problems arise then, this can lead to the rider holding on or even pulling with the reins, resulting in the full force of the pressure from the bit being felt on the horse's highly sensitive tongue.

If it is necessary why not change the position of your hands?

32

Whenever the position of the hands is debated, I always like to think of a cross country rider, who sits "classically" in a forward seat approaching a jump with his hands up on the neck in the mane, prepared at any time if things go wrong to change the position of his hands to rectify the situation. In other words – it is better to ride effectively than to hold the reins as if you were in a text book and hit a tree!

There isn't much to say about the aids through the seat, apart from them supporting the other aids. Knowing where you want to go should automatically result in the appropriate weight distribution.

When describing the application of the aids in a lesson, I always like to draw comparisons with western riding. There, the horse is taught in such a way that only a slight movement is necessary to ask for anything. Less is definitely more. In my opinion, learning a language is also a good comparison to using the correct aids. When starting out you will only be able to master a few words, and then only be able to say them hesitantly. You'd probably need an interpreter to help anyone understand you. The more words you learn though, the more confidently and expressively you can say them and then use them with more inflection and feeling.

Here is an appropriate place to quote from a conversation I had with Egon von Neindorff on the theme of feeling and perception:

"As an instructor I am well able to teach a rider everything. Feeling and empathy however, the rider must develop for himself. In this he is, just like the horse, both a recipient and giver. The reaction of my horse tells me which aids to use.
If you do not listen to nature you are making a grave mistake."

Egon von Neindorff

- **Half halt**

  The words imply coming halfway to the halt. In older editions of the German "principles", the definition for the half halt went in a similar direction: frame the horse as if you were going to ask for halt but continue to ride on. In my eyes this is a much more helpful description to a student than the usually heard "brace your back and keep an active seat and leg".

- **Build up the use of the leg**

  When applying the leg aid, don't start at force 5 when you only have 10. Begin gently, even questioningly. Pinter von der Aue in the seventeenth century spoke about the "leg that feels every hair and breathes with the horse". For me this is a good description, since it expresses exactly how the leg should be in contact with the horse: neither pressed in nor held away.

- **Letting through**

  In order to avoid over eagerness on the part of horse or rider, for example when lengthening, simply end the previous exercise, "let the aid through", and the lesson will develop by itself.

- **Send off, send away**

  This is the next stage up from "letting go". The leg is increasingly applied, building up (see above) or even more actively.

- **Asking, enquiring**

  Goethe wrote: "From heaven he demanded the most beautiful stars and from the earth the greatest desires". It shouldn't be like this when executing new movements or exercises. For me it is more a matter of being restrained when applying the aids, as this allows you to rethink the progression of the exercise if the horse doesn't immediately respond.

- **Offer, try**

  After an exercise is successfully established, weigh up whether or not you should consider asking for more.

- **Stretching**

  In German there are two words for stretching – "strecken" and "dehnen". The author prefers to use the second word as he extends the sound of the word out when he says it – like saying "stre-e-e-tch" as it says something about the time span involved when asking the horse to stretch down.

- **Free lines or tracks**

  This is what my father called riding off the outside track, or away from the usual schooling patterns. They serve to check the effectiveness of and connection between the aids, help in improving straightness but also help the instructor assess the horse and rider partnership on the day.

- **Kind lateral movements**

  Have in mind the concept of a lateral exercise that, when carried out, places more emphasis on the forwards rather than the sideways.

- **The value of recognition**

  Structure your lesson clearly and sensibly so that when learning something new, or when experiencing problems, you are able at any time to go back to an already well practised exercise.

- **Use your ideas, transmit your thoughts**

  Literally only take the idea of a new exercise forwards. Have a clear picture of the exercise in your mind, as Richard Hinrichs always maintains, and often that is enough. If necessary the transmission of your thoughts can also be supported through gentle aids.

Preparatory exercises: on the track of the lateral movements

Since the total package of all the lateral movements is very extensive and can be confusing, we are going to introduce exercises that lead up to the lateral movements to get us on the right track.

Preparation on the ground

Preliminary exercises on the lunge

Lungeing is a good way of schooling the horse without the added strain of the rider's weight. When lungeing I have the added advantage of being able to use circles of different diameters. By combining these with increased bending and extensions in a straight line, the transitions between a horse's ability to drive himself forwards and to carry himself can be practised.

You must however remember that due to the shape of the circle, the speed and the natural crookedness, a horse that is, for example, crooked on the right will balance themselves to the outside on the right rein and to the inside on the left rein.

The role of the person lungeing consists of working against this uneven strain, or more precisely to work on the added stress on the shoulders and the possible dropping of the vertebrae in the neck. In this way bending, stretching, engagement of the haunches and finally improved balance can all be achieved.

Typical starting out point: the vertebrae have dropped down between the shoulders.

This shows the correct position of the lunge line, the whip and the handler when working on the left rein.

36

We will next turn our attention to the actual process of lungeing, assuming that we undertake the appropriate warm up. On the left rein, take up the lunge line in the right hand. The line runs through my left hand up to the cavesson. My whip is also in the right hand and is held in such a way as to create a triangle between the quarters, the handler and the horse's head.

So that the horse can move freely and balance himself, I don't use side reins and just lunge off the lungeing cavesson. In this way the horse can find his own balance and gives me a more realistic picture of my work.

"Check, when someone ties down the horse's head, whether or not he can find a better way."

Friedrich Schiller

For my equipment I have a lunge line, a whip that can reach the horse, sturdy footwear, gloves and ideally also a riding hat to a minimum of the European safety standard. Don't forget about treats as well – whereby the use of them is too numerous to describe. My only tip would be – use sensibly.

On the left rein the sequence of events is as follows: start out at a walk. Then by asking gently through the lunge line, ask for bend towards the centre of the circle. At the same time point the whip towards the shoulder and if necessary flick the end of the whip to encourage the inside fore leg to lift. In a short time the horse should begin to take the weight off the inside shoulder and transfer more weight to the outside. The inside shoulder will become more supple, the circle will get bigger, and the bend will be easier to achieve. As you build up, shoulder-in should also be achievable.

Bending through the cavesson: by doing this the horse will become more supple.

If the horse is more balanced, you should be able to ask for some initial stretching.

Through targeted lungeing, the suppleness of the shoulder can be significantly improved.

If I get the smallest of reactions I recognise the effort by giving, and send the horse forwards on a straight line. If the horse falls in again on the shoulder then I go back on to the circle.

The aim is that the horse, as already described in the section "About the anatomy", lifts up through the shoulders and stretches. When going large he should be prepared to be sent on forwards in this outline and with the beginnings of self-carriage allow himself to then be called back again.

If I am faced with a horse that is extremely one-sided, then I do the following: in the case of a horse that is worse to the right, on the right rein I pay more attention to the hind leg that is wanting to move to the inside and think more about working the horse with his quarters out.

On the left rein, I concentrate more on the inside shoulder and consciously use my own body language to help correct him.

In canter the procedure is exactly the same. Here however you must remember that due to the increased speed there is more pull to the outside.

If you ask for too much the danger exists that the horse will lose his balance, pull against you or will fall out. In this case I will ask for less, allow the horse to canter more straight lines and work in short bursts.

"All methods of training that help us to understand the horse better should always be supported. The only thing to remember is – it shouldn't go so far as to be at the cost of riding itself!"

Helmut Beck-Broichsitter

At the end of the lesson I always let the horse stretch when going large, watching that the walk comes from the shoulder. This means, if he sinks down through the neck or gets too fast I ask immediately for the bend, without however asking too much.

In general, the principle applies of always asking for less than you think you are. It is always more strenuous at the other end of the lunge than you think it is from where you are standing in the middle.

Preliminary exercises in-hand

The horse is a herd animal. Even as a riding horse, it usually lives as part of a herd, with an inbuilt hierarchy: he will trust the other members of the herd and follow the herd leader. Using this herd instinct in your work with your horse is the ideal basis for systematic training. The horse should not view a person as an oppressor who takes away his freedom, or later even as a threatening predator on his back.

Working in hand offers the best opportunity to gymnasticise the horse with targeted exercises without the added burden of the rider's weight.

Training should instead equip a horse to both mentally and physically carry a rider.

There are diverse methods of training to reach this stage or at least lead in this direction. One extremely helpful method is the work in hand, which offers the chance of suppling the horse without the weight of a rider.

The advantages of working in hand are:

- The horse can be made more supple without the rider's weight interfering with him.
- The hierarchy between horse and handler can be established.
- Body language can be used in a way that is more targeted and with more awareness.
- Without the supporting weight of the rider and the leg and weight aids being involved, you become more aware of the aids through the rein.
- The work demands more from the horse mentally.
- The handler can immediately see how the horse moves and directly react when and where necessary.
- The horse is able to learn specific or new exercises in an easily understandable way.
- The horse is prepared for being ridden.
- The forehand and the hind quarters will become more supple.
- As you progress it is possible to do more advanced work on the lateral movements or in the initial steps towards piaffe.
- Old or ill horses can be gently exercised.

In order to avoid misunderstanding, knowledge of the horse's sight is of great benefit. The horse sees the area marked in green with both eyes and for this reason most clearly. He sees less clearly in the white area whilst things within the red area are in his blind spot. (Illustration: Mähler)

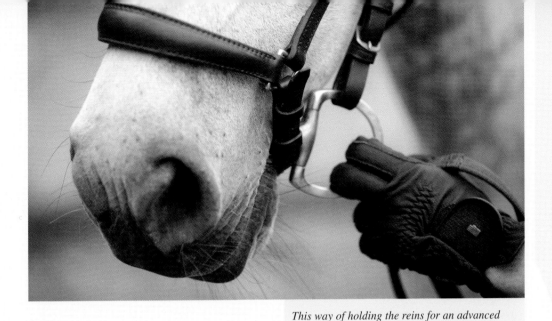

This way of holding the reins for an advanced handler allows a finer application of the aids.

I find the following a particular appropriate comparison: working in hand is like dancing. Only when there is a clear lead, can it be done well and be fun for both partners.

For an animal of flight such as the horse, in the wild it is a matter of life and death to be aware of his surroundings and, in the case of danger, being able to immediately run away. For this reason it is not only sensible, but helpful, for the stages of his ongoing training that he has a free head – or rather be in a position to freely move both head and neck from the shoulder.

This book is less about the equipment or the first steps in working in hand, but rather more it concentrates on the development of the lateral work in hand.

Important to this is the way you hold the reins. The inside hand holds the rein's buckle at the bit ring, with the fore and middle finger holding the bit ring itself. For those learning, for reasons of safety, only the buckle should be held. The advanced handler can have a differing effect with the fore finger but is aware of the dangers that exist if the horse throws his head up. In the case of a beginner who lacks this experience he can let the rein go more easily in a difficult situation.

Here the correct way of holding the reins is shown when using a double bridle for in hand work.

In order to create a contact through the outside rein, the outside hand holds the rein lying over the withers and takes it down to the inside until you can feel the mouth through the outside rein. The outside hand has a number of jobs. It has to give direction, control the bend, regulate tempo and in addition, if necessary apply the whip.

The whip should be held horizontal to the ground at a height level with the horse's elbow, but must not under any circumstances constantly be used or touch the horse, since action results in reaction. The whip should help to frame the horse and, as training progresses, to further activate the hind quarters.

Particular attention should be given to the position of your own body when working in hand. Only when I put myself in the right position and give clear signals can a horse distinguish them and react. Once you are used to each other, a slight turn of the shoulder should suffice to show where the next step goes. Always keep in mind the experienced dance couple.

If, despite everything, something goes wrong with either one of you then it doesn't matter. You don't have to be able to piaffe or complete the entire long side in shoulder-in. Two horses' lengths, or even initially the hint of a shoulder-in, are enough to start with. If then at some stage a few steps of piaffe are offered, delight in them, accept them and praise your horse.

Development of the lateral movements

- Ask for a series of upwards and downwards transitions from walk to halt at different points of the school. As you develop this, insist that the halt is square. If needed, use the whip quietly by touching the resting leg to square up.
- Use circles and voltes (6 – 10 m circles) to ask for increasingly more bend.

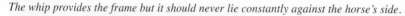

The whip provides the frame but it should never lie constantly against the horse's side.

Using the bend on a circle is a good way to develop shoulder fore. It is important to watch that the quarters don't fall out.

- Increase the bend on the circle until you are working in shoulder fore. The circle offers the advantage that the bend and direction of the movement are prescribed by the circle. If the horse falls out then you can immediately reduce the demands made. Go back to working large, in effect going back a step.
- Once the horse shows that he can cope with working on smaller circles then I will simply use this and transfer it to the long side of the school and work on shoulder fore or even shoulder-in.
- To keep his attention and the forwards momentum, always build in voltes every now and then.
- Use walk – halt transitions in shoulder fore as well to encourage the inside hind leg to step through and underneath.

Shoulder fore on the long side. Here though it is almost too extreme, with too much angle, and the foreleg is stepping too far into the school and off the track.

Out of the counter shoulder-in, as a result of the change of the bend and flexion comes ….

44

It is also possible to work on the travers as an in-hand exercise, for example out of the counter shoulder in. As counter shoulder-in and travers are virtually identical in terms of the direction of the movement and how the legs are placed, the only thing that is missing is the change of bend and flexion. In other words, this is the ideal prerequisite exercise for asking for travers. Whilst maintaining the bend, change the rein with the handler staying in exactly the same position. Without changing anything, the horse will now be doing a counter shoulder-in. Out of this, change the bend so that it is then bent in the direction of the movement and the horse will take up the travers.

Only go a few metres, otherwise the horse may lose his balance and fall on to the new inside shoulder. Practise this series of movements on both reins, taking regular breaks to allow him to stretch his neck.

Sometimes – assuming appropriate training – it is easy to develop out of the lateral work …

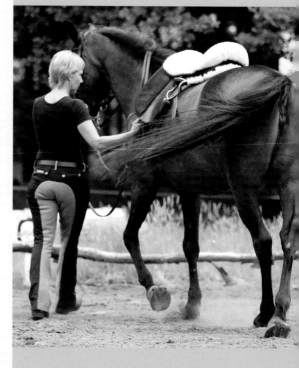

...the travers

This will suffice as a foundation to give the horse an idea of what the lateral movements are about as well as giving the handler a better picture of how supple the horse is and what difficulties it may have. Once the work is more concentrated it will not be long before you are able to carry out "kind" half passes and even renvers.

So that the forwards momentum isn't lost, start to include trot work. You must take into consideration though the fact that a horse at a normal walk is already moving faster than the rider walking beside him.

Added to this is the fact that (in the initial phases of training) the moment when he moves into trot will not be simultaneous with that of the handler. In order to avoid getting irritated, remember the importance of body language. Your body needs to say – if I trot

...the first piaffe

on, my horse will follow. What happens to the reins is secondary.

To move into the trot use, for example, the horse's natural desire to move forwards after coming to a halt and then backing up. Other moments that can be used are when you straighten up after shoulder fore or when you are enlarging the circle. In general you need to plan what you are doing carefully and tactfully, following the principle: if something is difficult, then I need to find something else that is harder, so that the first exercise appears easier. And again it should be a case of only asking for a few steps, not a marathon.

As training advances and once the trot is more secure, the same exercises done at a walk can be asked for in trot. But always remember, whilst enjoying the flexibility provided through using bend, you must always keep the forwards momentum as well as ensuring the horse continues to stretch.

At some stage the moment will come when the exercises that are well established can be worked at a shortened stride, moving towards collection. As Richard Hinrichs describes it, just ask for the movement "with no enthusiasm".

Problems and solutions

With in-hand work, we are also faced with the problems caused by natural crookedness or one-sidedness, which will result in the horse either sticking to the outside track or trying to come off the track to the inside.

How should this be overcome? In the case of the horse that is right-handed or crooked on the right, I will start out on the right rein. Here I use the ease of bending the horse to the right by repeatedly asking for bend up to shoulder fore on the circle. The horse will of course find this easier to do on the right hand than on the left. So that the bend is kept under control, only ask for it on the circle when returning to the track. Since it is in this type of horse's nature to step more through to the left rein, he offers himself more readily for shoulder fore down the long side. For a moment this will work, before the horse tries to balance himself back into his usual position of being heavy

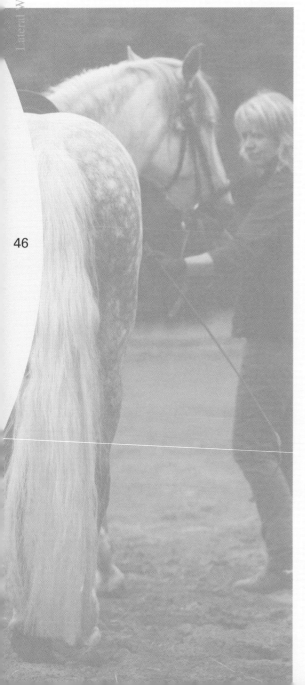

46

through the shoulder to the left, and refusing to take the weight through his right hind. Only then should you stop the exercise and try again.

On the left rein however I would do lots of turns, asking for bend to the left. On the circle I would also encourage the inside hind to use its natural flexibility and come through. I should have in my mind the hint of shoulder fore, almost as if I wanted to do a turn on the forehand with a bend, if necessary touching gently with the whip. From this I would go large, taking the bend through to shoulder fore. It will not be developed as much as was the case on the right rein.

Again I would only ask this for a few metres, and end the exercise before the horse runs out of steam and falls onto the left shoulder and shoves to the inside. In this way you are starting to stretch the right side whilst bending the left side, slowly but surely.

Further exercises involving, in quick succession, the need for pushing through and self-carriage, as well as bending and stretching, are all do-able. You should remember though that these exercises are more demanding of our four-legged friends than we, as two-legged beings, can imagine. Exercises to develop this further will be given for each of the different lateral movements.

Ridden preparation

Working on flexion and bending

After I have practised bending and flexing in-hand, I need to continue this work from the saddle. Begin in walk by riding large circles, later moving on to tighter turns and smaller circles. You should be aiming to supple the horse to prepare him for the lateral work to follow. The basic idea should be to introduce the horse to the approaching work with as long a neck as possible. To start with short reins would not only be bad for the horse mentally, since he will hardly be able to focus on the rider, but is immediately asking too much of him. In addition it is my goal that the horse develops a longer top line, bends and later is straight.

I work according to the principle: "what is long, can be bent; what is short, cannot be bent". As time progresses, the following also applies: "what is long can swing; what is short cannot swing". Thus we have a prescribed path to follow.

In order not to endanger the submission that has been achieved on circles and broken lines, I like to integrate an "in between" lesson that I call "carrying on the bend". This means that when riding out of the circle I keep in my mind the thought of maintaining a bend once back on the long side and going straight. The inside leg and the outside rein determine the straight ahead direction. The weight supports this and shows the rider the first hint of the use of weight in riding the horse with a bend but in a straight line, which is helpful when riding shoulder-in. If the horse finds this easy to do then it results in what my father called "rein balance". The outside rein stays in a soft contact, your outside leg causes the outside hind leg to step through into the contact. If necessary you can give with the inside rein in order to make it easier for the horse. And finally don't forget about the need to go forwards.

In terms of what you are asking, it is minimal – you could almost say that it only happens in the rider's mind. But even here, falling out through the outside shoulder, becoming crooked or problems with the contact can all effectively be avoided.

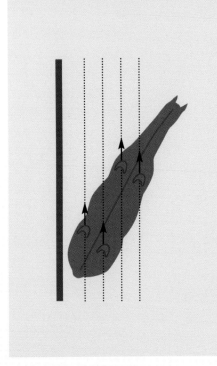 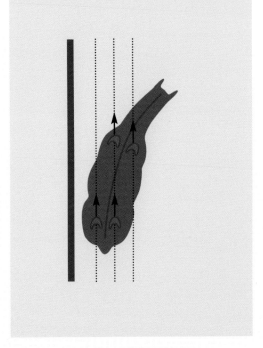

In comparison to shoulder-in (right), in leg yielding (left) the horse is not bent and the angle is greater.

48 Leg yielding

"My horse can do lateral movements: renvers, travers and leg yielding." This was the answer from a competition rider working at medium level to my question of what her horse could do.

Unfortunately though, leg yielding does not belong to the lateral movements, since the horse, whilst having slight lateral flexion through the jaw, should show no bend.

The horse moves forwards and sideways at an angle of usually at most 45 degrees on two tracks along the long side or on any straight line chosen. The inner legs just cross and step through past the horse's centre of gravity. In all its forms therefore leg yielding is primarily a loosening and warming up exercise.

It is however suitable for giving the first experience of lateral work, because the horse can get the feeling of crossing his legs without the added and more difficult demands imposed when bend is asked for. In addition, a rider who is learning this as well can get an idea of how all of the aids work together in getting the forwards sideways movements. I use leg yielding mainly though for beginners or to improve the understanding when learning other exercises. Since with leg yielding there is the danger that the horse bends through the neck, particularly here all aids should be viewed rather like questions. Only then is it possible for the exercise to be quickly broken off if difficulties arise.

In terms of the application of the aids, the reins show the forehand the desired angle, with the leg holding and guarding it. The outside rein provides support to prevent too great an angle or the shoulder falling out, at the same time ensuring, by giving the rein, the position to the inside. The inside rein accepts

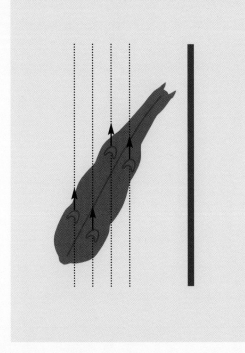 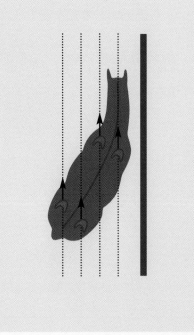

In comparison to travers (right), in leg yielding (left) the horse is not bent and the angle is greater.

the slight flexion and the softness. The inside leg that lies slightly behind the girth creates the forwards-sideways movement. The outside leg behind the girth guards against the quarters stepping around too much and maintains the forwards movement.

According to the German "Principles for riders and drivers", the rider's weight should be placed more on the side of the sideways driving leg. It is my opinion however that it is more sensible for the horse to step through under the weighted seat bone – in other words, put your weight to the outside towards the direction of the movement. Try thinking about a warrior fighting on horseback, who is trying to duck out of the way of his opponent.

He will try to get out of the way of danger by moving in the opposite direction of course. It is then only helpful if the horse has learnt to step under the transferred weight, rather than move away from it – otherwise

it could be painful, never mind lethal!

For the process of learning and further work in travers as a "real" lateral movement, I have though had good experiences with using leg yielding for horse/rider partnerships starting out. Since the angle is almost the same and the aids are similar, it offers a good opportunity to give a taste of the new exercise through the change of balance. To do this the rider must just ask for bend and flexion in the direction the horse is moving, and support the horse through the leg and seat. It must however only be a hint of a question, since most horses, due to the changed balance, are only able to stay in the new position for a short time and want to escape back into the old outline. Since the difference between the flexing and the bending of the neck is very slight, it is also very important to ask for less and above all place great importance on maintaining the forwards movement.

Shoulder fore

In trot I don't use leg yielding at all, not even on short stretches. The danger is too great, in my opinion, due to the sideways movements, for the horse to try to balance himself back towards the outside track. This frequently happens when you see too great a bend through the neck.

Shoulder fore

On the way to straightness and lateral work, shoulder fore and riding in position (or flexion), also known as the first and second positions, are two inescapable exercises that you cannot, and should not, avoid. Since the hocks are not capable, at the beginning of a horse's training, of carrying his full weight and accepting the full effects of the strain built up from the legs' bending, the shoulder fore helps by preparing first one then the other hind leg to take a greater load.

The ability to carry himself to the same degree through the hocks follows only at a later stage, when both sides are strengthened to the same degree. If you should try, despite this, to place the same amount of stress on both hind legs, in other words begin too early with collection, it will be made harder through the horse's one-sidedness, since one hind leg will push through whilst the other begins to carry.

The shoulder fore or – as my father rather more descriptively called it – "bringing the inside shoulder in front of the inside hip" demands, through the work moving from one side to the other, that the hind legs move in closer together, encouraging the hind legs to carry more weight. Remember that in the middle of the seventeenth century the Duke of Newcastle spoke of the horse's hind legs moving on a "narrow gauge".

Here you can clearly see that the right hind leg follows the right fore, whilst the left hind steps towards a point that is between the two front legs.

In addition the shoulder fore is used in the introduction and the conclusion of many lessons and exercises and prepares the horse for work moving from the outside to the inside track, without giving away the bend at the cost of the forwards movement or impulsion.

Since through systematic preparation horses can be taught shoulder fore fairly quickly, it is particularly important with young horses always to watch out that you ask for only a

Moving from trot to canter, using the sidewards bend of the shoulder fore is a particularly effective exercise. You can clearly see the outside hind leg strongly pushing off from the ground into an uphill canter.

few steps of a collected pace over a short stretch, in order to avoid overstressing or the horse resisting what is asked.

Should difficulties occur during training then you have in the shoulder fore a reliable correction exercise that you can return to again and again.

For the shoulder fore, the forehand is only brought in through the reins so far, to the inner edge of the outside track, for the inside shoulder of the horse to come just in front (i.e. to the inside of) of the inside hip. The inside hind leg steps towards a point between the fore legs, whilst the outside continues to step in line with the fore leg. The horse should be positioned and bent in the same way as if you were riding a 30 metre circle. The application of leg and seat comes automatically from this whereby more attention is given later to the subject of weight distribution. Anyone standing in front should clearly see only three legs.

When starting out, you should also recall the earlier exercise "keeping the bend". To advance this to shoulder fore all that needs to be done, riding out of a circle, is to lead more with the outside rein and let the sideways movement of the forehand take more of a front

Shoulder fore is ridden correctly when

… the rhythm remains regular

… the horse can at any time be asked to stretch and take the contact down.

… an improvement in the contact is noticed.

… the horse's forwardness is kept even when the tempo is being changed.

… there is an improvement in the ability to ride the horse between the hand and the leg.

… the inside hind leg bends and steps through more.

… you have the feeling that an entire long side can be ridden without losing rhythm, tempo, angle, bend or flexion.

… afterwards the trot feels more energetic.

If we increase the angle of the outside shoulder to the outside track sufficiently, such that the inside shoulder is positioned just in front of the inside hip, this determines the first degree of the bend through the body, whilst ensuring that the outside hind leg is not going to fall out. This positioning of the horse, which forms the foundation of all movements on circles or curved lines, whether on a single or double track, is described by us as shoulder fore.

Gustav Steinbrecht

seat. Now the inside leg faces its first main task: keep the forwards movement and drive the inside hind leg towards a spot in between the front legs. If you don't apply the aids correctly the usual result is that the horse takes up an angle that is more appropriate for the shoulder-in. At the same time you will also see a loss of tempo and rhythm. That is why here too the principle applies of asking for less than you think you need, as it is more effective than you think – less really is more.

Shoulder fore can be ridden on just about all the school figures. Those not suitable are when they don't allow you to ride forwards out of the exercise or if the horse doesn't trust himself to do this due to his lack of experience or limited field of vision. Examples of these are when you are riding into a corner or at the end of a long side.

Once the rider is confident in the exercise it can be used on the circle. Here you get the advantages offered by the circle on one side, and enjoy the benefits of the shoulder fore on the other. It is all about targeting work to achieve suppleness of the forehand, balance as well as encouraging the hind legs to cross over (something that they don't need to do when going straight).

Riding in position (flexion)

Just as with shoulder fore, riding in position serves to supple the haunches. Here though it is the outside hind leg that is being trained.

Through gentle flexion and bending to the inside, the horse's outside hind leg should step through to a point between the forelegs whilst the inside hind follows the inside fore. The rider should now, according to the riding instructions of 1882 "whilst sitting straight see the inside nostril and the glint of the eye".

Riding in position is an exercise that can hardly be seen. Here it is shown with almost too much stepping through of the outside hind leg.

An observer from ahead should see a glimpse of the hind leg between the front legs. In your mind's eye you should imagine a hint of travers, whilst staying on the outside track.

This exercise is often described as the position for canter, since the outside hind leg is being prepared for its future job of beginning the canter.

This position is less than you may want, but is more effective than you may also think. To avoid the danger of the horse going crooked or moving into a form of travers, it is particularly important to keep up the forwards momentum. As long as the feeling of the minimum position has been cemented, it is always helpful to have someone from outside offer correction. A mirror can be helpful but best of all is the critical eye of your instructor. Another effective help is a video recording of the legs.

To help develop this exercise, ride out of a 20 metre circle, keeping the same amount of bend. You should then be able to see both the horse's inside eye and inside nostril, and with the outside leg behind the girth, ask the outside leg to think about travers. And finally: forget about the aids and think forwards.

A comparison of shoulder fore and riding in position.
The main difference is the direction in which the hind legs move.

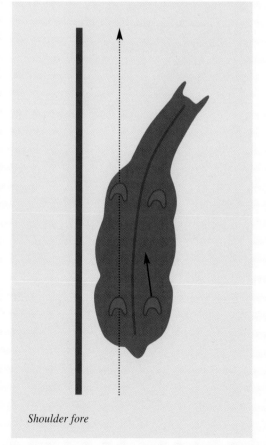

Shoulder fore

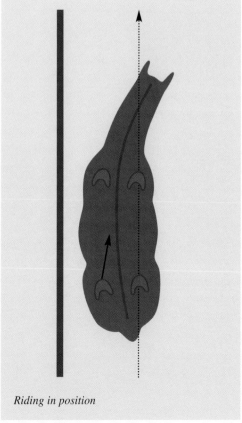

Riding in position

The lateral movements profiled

After the descriptions of the basics and the preliminary exercises, we are now moving on to what we think of as the true lateral movements: shoulder-in, travers, renvers and half pass, in which the emphasis should be placed on the shoulder-in and the travers. Both of these form the basis for any systematic training programme. In order to give the reader a clear structure and for ease of comparison, each of the following chapters is set out in a similar way.

Shoulder-in

Known as the mother of all lateral movements, the shoulder-in was described in detail by François Robichon de la Guérinière as "L'Epaule en Dedans" together with its gymnastic benefits.

However in 1600 the act of bringing in the shoulders on a volte, a type of a shoulder-in, had already been mentioned by Georg Engelhard von Löhneysen.

In comparison to the shoulder fore, the shoulders are brought off the outside track through increased bend and flexion, so that the outside foreleg moves in a line with the hind leg. The horse should move on three tracks at an angle of approximately 30 degrees from the edge of the school and is bent away from the direction of movement. Whilst the hind legs should virtually still move straight ahead, the fore legs cross over slightly due to the slight sideways positioning.

In what is known as the "Baroque" version of the shoulder-in as described by la Guérinière in his quote on page 59, the forehand is brought further over so that the horse is working at an angle of 45 degrees, similar to that attained during the leg yield, so that each leg

Shoulder-in

A comparison of shoulder-in: the Barock form on four tracks is shown on the left, whilst the right shows the three-track version more often used today.

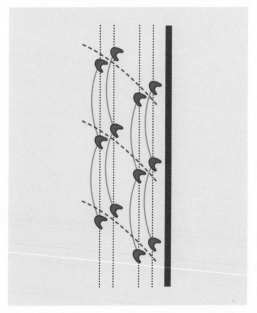
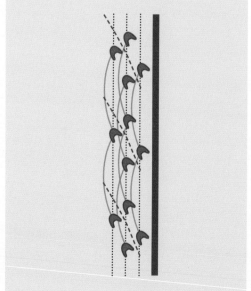

is working on its own track. The actual bend and flexion will be less than that of a three-track shoulder-in.

Modern opinion is that the collecting effect of the exercise is lost in the Baroque version, since the horse is actually stepping through, past his centre of gravity. This issue is not addressed in Baroque teaching since it does not differentiate between loosening and collecting exercises, as is the case today.

In the end, precisely which form of shoulder-in is actually ridden need not become

It should confine the front feet and place them in the correct place, it should be even and consistent, it should not run out through the quarters, but instead the hind feet should be placed in the middle of the track.

Georg Engelhard von Löhneysen

Instead of allowing the horse to go straight ahead when on the outside track with hips and shoulders aligned, place his head and neck a bit to the inside to point towards the middle of the school as if you were about to turn, and once it is angled and bent like this let him move forward along the outside of the school supported by the inside rein and leg. This lesson has so many good effects at once, that I view it as the most important of all exercises with which to make the horse totally supple and loose throughout all parts of his body.

François Robichon de la Guérinière

an ideological debate but should instead be a matter of doing what is most useful for the horse. Both forms can be a solution "for and against everything" and should not become something to argue about, but rather the reason for an open exchange of views and experience.

Its value as a gymnastic exercise and use in training

In the shoulder-in, the inside hind is encouraged to step more under the horse's centre of gravity. At the same time the hip and knee joints have to bend more (through the haunches) and the ability of the hind quarters to carry more weight is tested. In this way balance, straightness and collection are all improved. Obedience to the leg will be developed, because the horse must react more sensitively, improving his lateral bend. Due to the sideways crossing of the fore legs, in

connection with the increased bend through the haunches, the horse will become freer through the shoulder. The heightened attention and motivation that the horse develops can be increased even more through alternating with other lateral movements. The Portuguese Riding Master Nuno Oliveira described the shoulder-in appropriately as "the aspirin of the riding world, that cures everything".

Aids

The reins direct the forehand, the legs are responsible for controlling the quarters; the seat acts in a supporting role.

At this stage we should provide an initial and simple description of the aids. Further discussion of the use of the rider's weight through the seat and legs will be dealt with more exhaustively in the "Shoulder-in Special" chapter (from page 105).

Once horse and rider have prepared them-

The changing leg position (above on the girth: below behind the girth) is governed by the stage of training and the difference may only be a matter of a few centimetres.

selves for the exercise through a half halt, the horse is led into the exercise through both reins but primarily on the outside rein. The outside rein should allow the horse to bend sufficiently to the inside and allow the outside shoulder enough room to move forwards. In addition it works together with the outside leg that lies a hand's breadth behind the girth also controlling the bend. The inside rein receives the softness from the outside rein and ensures together with the inside leg that lies on the girth a smooth sideways movement and the flexibility of the horse, at the same time maintaining the forwards momentum and encouraging the inside hind to carry more weight.

Developing the exercise

In the initial work for shoulder-in, as well as, later, in the other lateral movements, I always keep at the front of my mind a very helpful suggestion from Egon von Neindorff (1923 – 2004). He recommended that I observe the following points in the following order, which reflects their relative importance: to build on the training scales in the order of rhythm, tempo, flexion, bend, and only then the angle of the body. If any one of these points suffer or are lost then you must immediately ask for less. If everything goes well, then you can easily ask for more.

Before starting the shoulder-in you need to check the horse's flexibility and the softness, or rather remind the horse about it. This can be done on a large circle or just beforehand on a volte. You take the bend with you out of this circle into the shoulder-in, albeit with more contact on the outside and if possible more enthusiasm and reaction to the forwards/side-

Working on the circle can help to improve the quality of the shoulder-in.

ways leg aids than the forwards aid alone. If in these initial stages the horse can hold the exercise for only a few horse lengths, then that is quite enough to start with. You should then straight away ride a circle, change the rein across the school or go into a rising trot in order not to over ask, and to highlight the importance of the forwards movement.

Out of this comes a series of exercises to form a lesson that will help to develop and improve the shoulder-in.

Circle at E or B – on the open circle side, ride shoulder fore (you are preparing the bend and the inside hind leg for the next request) – then go large and ride shoulder-in down the rest of the long side.

Reduce the size of the circle – then in shoulder fore make the circle bigger again (freeing up the inside shoulder) – go large and continue in shoulder-in.

Voltes along the long side (continuously checking the bend and changing the weight through the seat) into shoulder-in.

On the long side shoulder fore (to secure the bend) – circle with shoulder-in on the open circle side.

Typical mistakes and corrections

In order to avoid mistakes and to avoid learning bad habits a rider should always be satisfied with the smallest of achievements. Of course he should always ask what is required, but only for short bursts. This ensures that he receives the horse's full attention, maintains his motivation, avoids overtaxing the horse and prevents the pair getting too tired. At the same time you must consider whether any mistakes that occur do so at the moment of a problem occurring and for obvious direct reasons or whether they are caused somewhere else.

Below highlighted in brief are some of the small "irregularities", as I like to call them, their typical causes, and suggested sensible ways of solving the problem.

In general, in the case of problems, the rule is – do less, in case of doubt stop the exercise and continue in rising trot to encourage the horse forwards and if necessary re-establish the contact.

62

Here the shoulder-in shows the quarters falling
out – you can see this by the way the outside hind is
moving, with the leg tending towards the outside.

Produced especially for this photo, incorrect placing
of the rider's seat leads to a common mistake:
the bend is totally lost from the shoulder-in.

Typical mistakes in the shoulder-in.

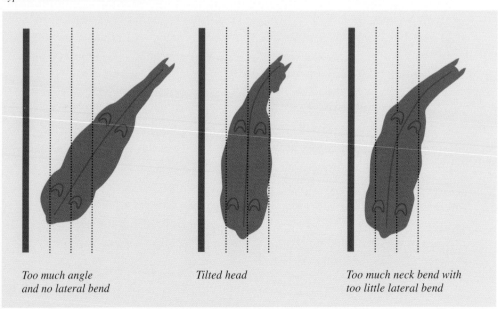

Too much angle
and no lateral bend

Tilted head

Too much neck bend with
too little lateral bend

Possible problems – horse	Possible causes	Solutions
Irregular rhythm, varying speed	• Loss of balance, lacking freedom through the shoulder. Only having neck bend.	• Lighten the inside hand and use the inside leg to re-create forwards movement.
Losing submission	• Too much emphasis is often placed on active hind legs at the cost of maintaining the forwardness whereby the actions of pushing and carrying often don't fit together.	• Stop the exercise • Convince the rider of the benefits of less is more • Re-establish the lateral submission by using serpentines • Reduce activity by using counter shoulder-in
	• Too much is asked, for too long	• Don't fall into the trap of wanting to ride the exercise for the length of the long side; instead divide it up into shorter stretches
Falling out through the hind quarters	• The hind legs aren't up to the demands being placed on them and try to avoid the effort	• Use travers to prepare for the exercise and then think travers when shoulder-in • Use figures of eight (changes the outside hind to become the inside and must bend)
	• Too much inside hand or leg is used, or rider is collapsing through the inside hip	• Ride on an inside track in a counter-position or bend or even think of riding renvers.
Problems with the contact (tilting head or behind the vertical)	• Using too much hand: fixing, "riding backwards", causing the horse to seek to change his balance.	• Ride circles with a sideway guiding hand • Ride with one hand • Imagine allowing the horse to take the reins down and stretch • In your mind be able to think "relax"
Too much angle and not enough bend	• The horse sets himself or the rider has the wrong idea of the angle that is required	• Try riding travers, voltes or figures of eight
Horse becomes unsettled or restless	• Horse is being asked for too much or horse and rider lose track of what they are trying to achieve	• Ask for the exercise on different lines but to a lesser degree. Halt frequently and take time to rest

Possible problems – rider	Possible causes	Solutions
The exercsie is not ridden clearly	• The rider has the wrong picture in his mind of what is being ridden	• The instructor's job is to chose a different explanation or show how it should be ridden; ask for only a few metres to be ridden possibly at walk
Collapsing through the hip	• The horse's shoulder may not come away from the outside of the school or the inside leg is edging into the inside	• Ride serpentines paying attention to the turns, reverting to rising trot thinking more about the forwards movement than the angle
The inside hand crosses over the withers or is having a backwards action rather than allowing forwards	• Lacking softness	• Hold the reins further apart, or use the whip as an aid to keep your hands apart (see photo below)
Instead of shoulder-in, "head-in" is ridden with neck band	• Too much inside rein	• Imagine you are neck reining (coming from western riding, the ouside rein is pressed against the neck) • Sit more to the inside
	• Rider is sitting too much to the outside and collapsing through hip	• Use counter shoulder-in to improve the rider's execution of the exercise • Bring the rider's outside hip more underneath the body. Put more weight down through the inside of the stirrups

A good exercise to correct hands that try and cross over the withers.
The whip helps to immediately show up any change in the position of the rider's hands.

Advanced variations

In order to keep the horse fresh and his attention focused on the shoulder-in, as well as to use the suppling effect for the benefit of other movements, I have developed a series of effective exercises throughout my riding and teaching career which I would like to share with you.

Firstly you should remember that shoulder-in can be ridden on a wide variety of lines, for example on circles, large and small, down the centre line, through the corners of the school, on serpentines ... in short, everywhere where the aids for the shoulder-in can be clearly understood by the horse and clearly given by the rider. (After Burkhard Beck-Broichsitter.)

* To create softness and activity through the inside hind, intersperse the shoulder-in with 6 – 10 metre circles. Maintain the bend on the circles, even possibly with the thought of quarters out. This will make the "simpler" bend asked for in the shoulder-in on a straight line easier for the horse.
* When changing from the circle to the straight line, be conscious of your balance and experiment with your seat and weight aids as well as asking for increased bend.

Shoulder-in using only a neck ring: this is a good way of checking if the rider really understands the concept of the movement.

Shoulder-in is ridden correctly when...

... at any stage I can vary angle, straightness and speed.
... I can ride the exercise with my horse on the aids on any line of my choosing and be able to change the line when I want.
... I can add any half pass movement to the exercise.
... I can further develop extension and collection out of the shoulder-in.
... afterwards, the trot is more expressive, elevated and has more impulsion.
... I can ride it with only a neck ring.

Riding corners can be improved through the selective use of the shoulder-in.

An example of this could be: at the start of the long side ride shoulder fore – volte – shoulder-in: change the rein using a half circle in the corner coming back to the school before E/B – shoulder-in: later try shoulder-in – volte – travers.

- The riding of corners can be specifically structured using the shoulder-in, the result of which is to improve the shoulder-in. One possibility is to ride through the corner in shoulder-in as if you were riding a half pirouette with forwards movement. The historical Prussian riding regulations (RR) from 1825 state: "The rider must, when riding through the corners in shoulder–in, ensure that the horse performs a continuous turn on the quarters with a mobile turning point. The inside hind should however never stop moving."

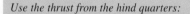

Use the thrust from the hind quarters:

Extended trot can easily be developed out of the shoulder-in.

Steinbrecht pleaded against riding through the entire corner in shoulder-in. "The old masters did not always ride the corners on two tracks, but instead used them to collect their horses by one to two lengths before the corner, reverting back to riding on the one track and restricting the bend of the shoulder-in through the corner. The inside rein and leg asked for the moving in of the forehand and hind quarters into the corner with the outside rein and leg leading out of the corner and back into the shoulder-in after the corner."

A well known variation in the nineteenth century was to ride a turn on the forehand out of the shoulder-in in the corner (Prussian RR from 1825): "The rider keeps the horse in the existing flexion until he reaches the corner, he then shortens up the horse in front whilst he asks for the hind legs to step underneath him

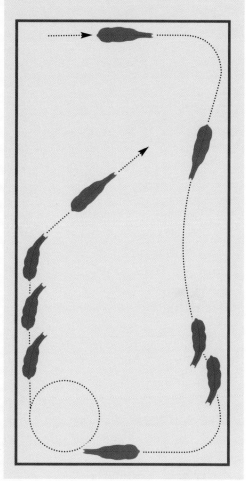

Transitions in quick succession with the shoulder-in as the main element will train co-ordination and both the carrying power and the driving power of the hind legs.

more through the corner until the horse comes onto the new line". The following quote comes from the RR of 1882 "whilst maintaining the flexion, two strides before reaching the short side, the reins ask the forehand to shorten. The hind legs step in the same rhythm around the forehand".

• At the start of the long side ride a few metres in shoulder-in and then change the rein across the "late" diagonal, asking for some lengthened strides. Here I am using the fact that in the shoulder-in there is less

The lateral movements profiled

weight on the forehand so with the forward thrust coming from behind, the legs are bent more, the horse is collected and is just waiting to be able to turn this thrust into forwards impulsion.

- The following exercise offers a way of increasing the demands asked of the driving and carrying ability of the haunches, as well as asking for greater concentration through the use of quick transitions: on the right rein begin the long side in shoulder-in for a few strides, moving late on to the diagonal as if changing the rein across the diagonal, let the strides lengthen as the horse is able, but only until reaching the centre line, there ride up the centre line in collected trot, taking up shoulder-in left until reaching the middle of the short side.

The positive effect of this exercise is the recognition value that it contains. This means that the horse will move forwards into the shoulder-in as he will suspect that the medium or extended trot may follow.

- A continuation of this exercise: in the shoulder-in the inside hind leg (in our example on the right rein) steps more under the centre of gravity, in other words he is already used to work where he is taking more weight through his hind leg. After the extension has fired the horse's enthusiasm, instead of moving into shoulder-in on the centre line, ride travers left (i.e. in the direction of the movement), whereby what was previously the inside hind is asked to cross over. This sequence of movements can of course be done on the other rein. By doing this type of exercise you are continuing to encourage as well as ask for more in terms of the horse's outline and obedience without the help of the outside edge of the school.

A good example: the half pass can be developed out of the shoulder-in.

- As a further development of this: after the shoulder-in, you can later add a half pass. The bend and the angle are already established and since the horse is familiar with the sequence of movements in the exercise he will know what direction is going to be asked for and should maintain his forwardness.
- Here too there is an additional level that can be tried: ride shoulder-in on the right rein – move on to the diagonal with extended trot – shoulder-in or travers on the centre line – at the middle of the short side left rein – from the beginning of the long side, half pass to the left.
- As a collecting exercise with clear demands for flexion of the inside hind leg, walk-trot transitions can be ridden in shoulder-in, both on straight lines and on circles.

Horses that, for example, like to lean through transitions will become lighter due to the increased transfer of weight to the outside, lifting up in front and become more mobile through the neck and shoulder.

In addition this exercise serves well as a preparation for shortening the stride working towards piaffe. Due to the transition when the horse is bent, more demands are placed on the flexion of the inside hind leg. If in the future the shoulder-in in trot is ridden to a stage when the horse is almost in walk, then the horse will anticipate the transition and slow down. Before he walks however he must immediately be sent forwards. Increase the demands further by building in the rein back. In this way you are increasingly integrating the horse's desire to go forwards into his work. With this I will later have another exercise which has "recognition value". This means: should the horse

suddenly not be able to carry himself or I need more expression in his movement, I only need to hint at shoulder-in and he should react immediately.

- For a secure and correct transition to canter: ride a five metre loop down the long side in shoulder-in and on reaching the track, still in shoulder-in, canter on. As you approach the track the outside hind is prepared for its task in the canter due to the increased weight it takes up in the movement. It should, descriptively put, push the whole horse from the outside hind to the inside fore. Thanks to the slight shift of the rider's weight to the outside which is required, the horse's inside shoulder becomes freer and can reach more forwards in the canter.

As a preliminary exercise the five metre loop in shoulder-in should be ridden firstly in walk, in order to also develop the canter from walk. With horses who have not done this before and may not be collected enough, it is a good idea to do a "dry run" and ride the loop simply in walk to get the line right. Later when practising, try shortening the loop up, i.e. come back to the track earlier than you normally would (a few metres before F, M, H or K). This means that the horse that is still learning not only has enough room to find his rhythm but the approaching short side will act as a brake on his forward movement.

A similar exercise that is just as effective for the canter transitions can be done on the circle approaching the track. The horse is already bent so you must just ask for a bit more and watch out that you assume the shoulder-in position. This encourages a rather better transition through from behind.

69

Counter shoulder-in

70

Counter shoulder-in

Counter shoulder-in is the opposite to the "true" shoulder-in. It is usually ridden on an inside track (i.e. off the outside track) with the forehand bent and flexed to the outside track. As with the shoulder-in, the haunches stay on the same track. The horse is therefore not bent towards the inside of the school but rather to the outside. (Which then becomes the inside, since the side to which the horse is flexed and bent is always referred to as the inside.)

The counter shoulder-in can be ridden on any straight line, but as training progresses, also on circles, or by treating the manège as an oval, also around the school.

Its value as a gymnastic exercise and use in training

Riding the shoulder-in involves playing with the sense of balance of both horse and rider. It is important to do this so the horse too develops his own balance. If I were to loose school a horse, a young horse or one experiencing difficulties with his balance is more likely to try and balance himself to the outside rather than to the inside.

As a rider, I should use this fact when preparing for movements or when encountering problems in training. If a horse becomes excited or I lose his attention then, as first aid at the scene of the accident so to speak, I can get him to focus back on me by changing the balance and the direction in which he is looking.

At the same time the counter shoulder-in allows me to swap over the demands I am making on the horse's inner and outer mus-

Counter shoulder-in on straight and curved lines – a game of balance.

Counter shoulder-in on a circle to the right. The rider is correctly looking towards the right.

Counter shoulder-in on the right rein.

culature: this can be very helpful when facing problems on circles in shoulder fore or shoulder-in. A tense or over stressed inner side that is bending to the inside of the school can be stretched by the counter movement, freeing up the muscles from the strain the exertion has produced.

In due course it is also sensible to do this exercise on the circle. Here the counter shoulder-in is particularly well suited to encourage collection, since the hind legs have to be able to cover varying distances.

The leg nearest the outside of the school is now the inside leg but has more ground to cover. This means that not only does it have to flex but it also has to reach forwards in order to stay in rhythm. For the new outside hind leg

(the leg nearest to the centre line) this also means, due to the shorter distance it moves, more flexion.

Finally, the counter shoulder-in is a good means to check and improve balance and the horse's attention as well as whether he is truly on the aids.

Aids

The aids are the same for the rider as in shoulder-in. On circles it may be necessary to make the weight transfer towards the direction of the movement more obvious, i.e. towards the outside (away from the direction of the bend) in order to prevent the horse trying to move over towards the outside of the track.

The lateral movements profiled

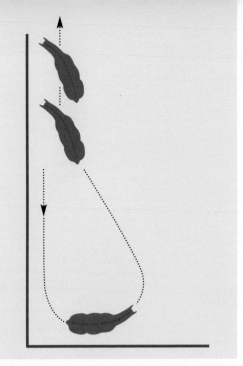

This shows how you can develop the counter shoulder-in through the corner in a half ten metre circle and back to the track.

Developing the exercise

Riding on the inside track the horse should be bent to the outside as if you were going to ride a volte in this direction, but instead ride straight ahead. The exercise can also be developed by changing the rein across half the school or out of the circle without changing the bend. A further variation is to ride a half 10 metre circle in one of the corners and before getting to the outside track straighten up and ride parallel to the outside track. To make it even harder, ride the exercise through the corners.

Advanced variations

- Counter shoulder-in – half ten metre circle in the corner back to the track – shoulder-in. The bend is the same.
- Counter shoulder-in – straighten for a few strides – forwards into canter. This is helpful

for preparing for the canter because in counter shoulder-in the inside hind leg (the one closest to the outside track) is flexed and is the one that starts the canter as the new outside leg. In addition the outside shoulder is freer in counter shoulder-in and can reach forwards more easily as the new inside shoulder. For a horse that is stiff to the right this exercise, for example, is very useful on the left rein in order to better prepare for the left canter that is often harder.

- Shoulder-in – change the rein – counter shoulder-in (keeping the bend and flexion) – straighten and lengthen stride. This is a good exercise to maintain the softness and to activate more flexion in what was previously the inside hind leg. Especially in turns, the hind leg has no other choice – in a positive sense – than to follow because it has to move further and in addition step

The counter shoulder-in…

Counter shoulder-in is ridden correctly when…

…due to the diverse questions asked of his hind legs, my horse feels more active and responds directly.

…I can steer my horse securely through all the movements.

…his paces become more expressive and energetic.

…his attention to the inside and outside aids is improved.

…he seeks the rein and moves up into it when straightened.

under the centre of gravity. Out of this you can develop his straightness and lengthened strides on the long side, starting on the path towards self carriage, impulsion and submission.

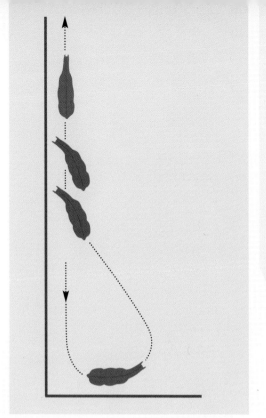

After counter shoulder-in ask for some lengthened strides – this is good for building up impulsion.

…is good for preparing for an energetic transition into canter.

Travers

Travers

The term travers comes to us from the French, with "en travers" meaning diagonal and "de travers" crooked or angled. The horse is thus positioned diagonally and he is moving at an angle to the track. Interestingly in France the movement is not called travers but instead "Tête au mur" (head to the wall) and "Croupe en dedans" (quarters in). The term quarters in is sometimes used as a synonym for travers and is perhaps easier to comprehend for a rider learning it for the first time.

In contrast to shoulder-in on three tracks, where it is only the forelegs that cross over and the hind legs virtually move straight ahead, in travers and its partner movement, renvers, both the fore and hind legs cross. This makes it a harder movement, demanding more especially of a horse's balance and should only be started when the shoulder-in is secure and – almost more importantly – when the rider, riding a straight line, can send the horse forwards when required.

In travers the horse is clearly bent and flexed in the direction of the movement. The forehand remains on the track whilst the hind quarters are brought off the track to the inside far enough that the outside hind steps on a line to the inside of the inside fore. At an angle of about 30 degrees the horse should therefore go on four tracks. To prevent the mistake of too great an angle and too little bend, it is advisable to start out by asking for less angle.

Riders learning this ask mostly for too much angle with too little bend (see also the details on page 77.)

When riding instructors hear a delighted pupil exclaim: "My horse can already do travers on one rein", it is unfortunately usually countered by the instructor saying, "No, he is just not going straight".

Since in travers the quarters are brought into the school, this is similar to the position a one-sided horse takes up on his stiff side. Therefore it is important to ensure that the horse is moving forwards well and that you have an awareness of what his hind legs are doing as a foundation for any further work.

As an internal snapshot, the rider needs to imagine that a picture is taken from above of only the horse's head and the headpiece of his bridle on the outside track. You should not be able to tell whether you are riding travers, circle or just going large. If this is not the case, then the instructor above would be right.

Its value as a gymnastic exercise and use in training.

As with the shoulder-in, in travers more is asked for in terms of the flexion and the ability of the inside hind leg to bear more weight. The outside hind will be asked to cross over more in front of, and over, the inside. As a result – according to the stage of training of the individual horse – there will be a greater bending through the haunches, more freedom through the shoulder and along with that, the forehand will become lighter and there will be a degree of greater collection.

The difference from shoulder-in consists of the bend being in the direction of the movement – a fact that contains advantages, as the curved sideways movement of the travers requires a different balance to all of the other movements that the horse has learnt to this stage. Should it not be prepared for carefully enough, the horse will try to find his own natural balance, which will be in opposition to the direction of movement.

With appropriate and careful progression, travers can also be used with advanced horses as a warm up exercise. For such horses it is also suitable as a preparatory lesson for collection of the canter.

Aids

The aids from the leg for travers are not markedly different from those used for the shoulder-in. There is a bit more of a difference in the role of the outside rein. It needs to be given enough – in co-ordination with the inside rein – in order to allow the horse to bend but still keep a strong enough contact to be able to lead the horse down the outside of the school as if along a railing. It is supported by the outside leg that should lie just behind the girth. The inside leg lies on the girth and is responsible for the bend and maintaining the forwards movement. It is the job of the weight, placed to the inside and forwards, to support the horse's movement underneath the rider's weight.

Travers (left) and renvers (right) are in principle identical – it is just the wall that has changed sides.

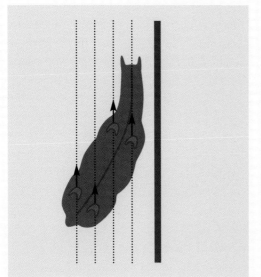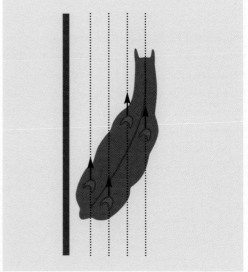

Some horses tend to want to try to edge back to the outside of the school, or even don't want to leave it at all. Here it may be helpful for the rider to think of shoulder-in when riding travers (and the other way around, i.e. of travers when riding shoulder-in). The rider's concentration and attention in travers is not fixated so much on the hind quarters, but rather achieves freedom through the shoulders (the other way around, in shoulder-in the rider will be thinking about the outside hind).

Developing the exercise

To avoid asking too much, and thus the mistakes that arise out of doing this, it is helpful to apply the aids in small steps.

It has proved useful to do an exercise where the bend out of a circle is continued on the long side and then a bit more angle is asked for. At the same time the outside hind leg has to be told in the corner by the rider's outside leg behind the girth, that it doesn't even want to think about returning to the outside track, but instead stay on the inside of it. It is then necessary to think about maintaining the forwards movement with the inside leg. (Of course it is always important to think of going forwards. For the sake of learning this movement though, I suggest working in the described sequence.)

Since at the beginning of the lateral work the horse is unlikely to be capable of the degree of bend asked for, the work in flexion (or position) is perfect to introduce the movement. This may also be called a mini-travers. As described on page 54 the horse is asked for minimal bend and flexion since the outside hind is asked to only move to a line between the fore legs. I would ask this to be ridden at a collected pace, without

The travers can be developed using this lesser known exercise, by which you change the rein out of a circle ridden into the corner.

losing sight of the forwardness of the movement – I would even get the horse moved on forwards every now and again to check this.

It is also easy to ride the travers using a school figure that is unfortunately less well known – see illustration above. This figure involves leaving the track to ride a half circle against the direction you have previously moved in, changing the rein in effect back into the corner. This has the advantage of creating the required bend with the hind legs already positioned to the inside of the track.

Typical mistakes and corrections

As with the shoulder-in it is necessary to pay most attention to not asking for too much, too soon. Only ride the travers in short stretches. In between, the horse should again and again be ridden forwards and allowed to stretch, interspersing sitting with rising trot. If pro-

blems arise too often then chose a different method, or reconsider whether the horse is ready for this movement in terms of his training and balance. If this is the case then it is better to return to the previous exercises and secure these once again. Although all of the mistakes that are mentioned are undeniably connected to each other and shouldn't be seen in isolation, I will list them individually for the sake of greater understanding.

Possible problems – horse	Possible causes	Solutions
Irregular rhythm, varying speed	• Too much angle asked for • Lacking freedom through the shoulder (inner shoulder may be blocked) • Loss of balance	• Ask for less angle, more bend and forward impulsion • Become lighter with the inside hand then ask more forwards with the inside leg
Too much angle, too little bend	• Aids are too strong • The rider has the wrong picture in his mind's eye • No sideways movement is shown	• Develop the travers along the long side • The riding instructor needs to find a different way of showing the pupil what is required, otherwise only work on the movement on one rein • Use circles, figures of eight, shoulder fore and counter exercises
No freedom in the shoulder, suppleness is lost, falling through the outside shoulder	• The inside rein is asking for too much bend • Outside leg is asking too much • Collapsing through the inside hip (when asking for the quarters to move in)	• Think of giving more through the rein or even think more of riding the horse straight • Think about doing less • Step more into the outside strirrup, ride a 6–10 m circle to the inside
Tilting the head (or similar problems with the contact)	• Loss of balance	• Given with the rein on the side the horse is tilting towards • Include circles in the work • Ask for less

Possible problems – rider	Possible causes	Solutions
Collapsing through the hip	• Trying to push the horse across with the seat	• Bring the outer hip more underneath the body • Ride without stirrups, with frequent changes between travers right and left
Outside shoulder stays too far back	• The outside leg and rein are not used independently of each other	• Learn to correct the various parts of your body individually • Build into your training lots of turns. Using the rein in the outside hand only. Neck reining (see box on page 64)
Inside leg is too far back, rider's weight is wrongly applied	• The horse's inside hind isn't quite ready for the demands being asked and tries to avoid the aid. Possibly puts the rider in the wrong position	• Try riding voltes (6–10 m) so that the calf goes back onto the girth • Ride shoulder fore on a circle, and include riding in flexion as well
The inside hand drops	• Rider has the wrong idea of required bend • Too much outside leg is compensated by the horse becoming straighter	• Hold the whip horizontaly between both first fingers to make you more aware of what the hands are doing • Take time to build the travers along the long side • The instructor can stand at a point in the school that shows the required degree of bend

Travers is ridden correctly when...

... the angle of bend can be varied at any time, without losing either rhythm or tempo.

... suppleness and looseness are always at hand, by for example going back to rising trot.

... the contact becomes lighter, but is still secure.

... the outside hind begins to become more active.

... the horse allows himself to be contained, is in front of the aids and can be directed in the direction of the rider's chosing.

... the outside shoulder can be moved away from the edge of the manège.

... I have the feeling that I could ask for canter by just shortening up the reins slightly.

... the horse carries himself through turns.

... as a result of the movement the basic paces have become more expressive and balanced and the horse swings through his back more.

... you can start easier forms of the half pass in conjunction with the travers.

... afterwards, in the shoulder-in, it is easier to keep the outside hind leg in position.

... later, as different lateral movements are ridden, I can alter my balance without difficulty.

Advanced variations

The travers can be ridden on straight lines or circles and other bent lines, and as training advances can also be ridden away from the outside track and thus without the support of the outside edge of the school. By riding alternately with the other lateral movements or exercises you will keep the horse's attention and increase his readiness to work.

The following exercises (in which the travers should be ridden in trot or initially perhaps in walk) have worked very well for me when teaching riders:

- The well known sequence of shoulder-in – volte – travers – volte – shoulder-in will improve the horse's obedience to the leg, attention, balance and suppleness and sub-mission.
- Since in travers the horse carries more weight through his haunches, travers is helpful as a preparation for a correct and quiet transition into canter. To be exact: the outside hind that begins the canter steps is more underneath the horse in travers and the inside hind, which in canter should step well through towards his centre of gravity, will in travers be flexed more and at the same time loosened. This link can be used to your advantage as follows: circle at A or C – on the open side travers – on the closed side (i.e. as you reach the track) canter on. Or: circle at B or E – travers on the circle – a length before reaching E or B, canter. In both of these exercises the horse should be straightened once in canter.

Another exercise: circle – travers (in trot or walk) – canter maintaining travers – transition to trot or walk, again maintaining travers. For the purpose of this exercise you should keep the horse in travers in canter.

This shows a frequent error in travers: the rider has collapsed through her hip, as a result altering the aid given through her seat.

79

By riding travers before canter the hind leg, that starts the canter…

Rider and riding instructor must however keep in mind that the horse too easily gets used to cantering "crooked" on two tracks when you don't want him to. It is therefore wise to intersperse this exercise with stretches where the horse is asked to canter in shoulder-in. By riding working canter on the circle, shortening the canter up in travers and then back to a working canter with the horse straightened, horses will find it easier to collect in canter because in travers the quarters are being asked to carry more weight.

- When cantering from travers, the more advanced rider can try altering the aids given through his seat (a là Philippe Karl): in the exercise from travers to canter, a movement is created in which the horse, in effect, is asked to move as if going "uphill". At the moment of the beginning of the

A helpful picture, showing how the canter out of the travers pushes the horse "uphill".

…is already underneath the horse's body and can perform its job more easily and with more power.

canter transition the inside leg is free to step through and forwards into the canter. If the rider moves his weight to the outside-back then he is encouraging exactly this sequence of actions. The inside shoulder, in particular, is freer to reach forwards than when the rider is placing his weight on to the inside and forwards. This variant of canter transition also has the advantage that the horse will be able to more easily differentiate between the aids to canter (with the weight to the outside) and the aids for half pass (weight to the inside) and so avoid confusion.

• Once I have secured the travers along the long side, I would then change the rein out of a half circle (6-10 metres) in the corner, keeping the bend of the travers until reaching the track. In other words, I am

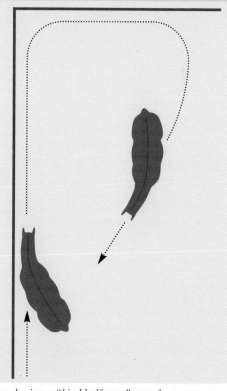

Developing a "kind half pass" out of travers.

The lateral movements profiled

starting to work towards the half pass.

I refer to a very small sideways movement like this as a "kind half pass", since at this early stage I deliberately place more importance on the horse finding the right direction and keeping his forwardness than on him crossing over his legs correctly. If a rider can then control the outside leg he will get his half pass.

In this strenuous position the horse will want to get back to the track quickly, so it proves best to ride half pass like this for only a few metres and then to go straight, and only then to move back into half pass. Through this rapid sequence you are constantly asking the horse to change his balance. The horse should stay focused and his muscles relaxed. Furthermore, the rider will learn to use the position that is so necessary for the half pass (with the rider's shoulders and hips parallel to those of the horse).

Small bites are easier to digest for both horse and rider, and better to absorb than when trying to suddenly ride the half pass from one side of the school to the other.

- The same exercise can be made harder or easier by changing the rein out of the corner in travers. In returning to the track it is important to think about sending the forehand out in front. The advantage for the horse and rider is that the aids for the bend and the direction of the movement stay the same and there is little risk that the inside hind leg is ignored.

- As a preparation for the canter pirouette, the circle in canter travers can be reduced down to a volte sized circle (6–10 metres). Ride out of the circle then in a straight line still in canter. Later the volte in canter travers can be reduced down until it becomes a

Proceed in small steps: when beginning to ride half pass only do it for a few metres, straightening up in between.

Antoine de Pluvinel shows King Louis XIII how he can turn on the spot in canter. (Drawing: Cadmos Archive.)

pirouette. This exercise was described in the seventeenth century by Pluvinal as riding travers around a pillar:

"**R**eversing the haunches so it is against the pillar, making a small circle in order to half pass around it, is an action whereby the horse learns to turn on the spot, which has increasing use in war; if one gets into difficulties it is then easier to extricate oneself and rescue yourself with the help of your horse."

Antoine de Pluvinel

Out of travers in canter the pirouette can be developed bit by bit.

The lateral movements profiled

Changing from travers…

into renvers has a particularly good suppling effect.

Travers or renvers? The only difference is in the direction the horse is moving.

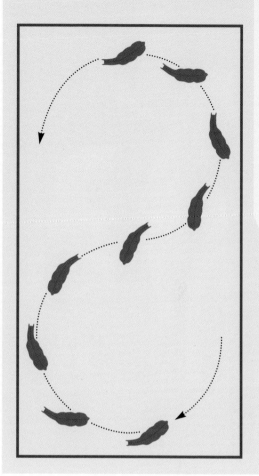

- A particularly good suppling exercise for the (old and new) inside leg involves a combination of travers and renvers on circles or serpentines. (See illustration above). In travers change the rein out of the circle without changing the bend or flexion and this becomes renvers on the next circle.

Then again change out of the circle back into travers. The inside hind leg, which in travers has to already flex more then in renvers, not only has to flex but also has further to travel and must reach forwards more in order to maintain the rhythm.

- To increase the difficulty further in terms of balance, obedience to the leg and keeping the flow, the same series of movements can be ridden on a figure of eight. Travers on the long side, in the middle of the long side ride a half ten metre circle to the right, change the rein over at X, continuing in renvers.

Change back into travers on the long side and enjoy the feeling that the horse's softness and suppleness has given you!

Renvers

The term renvers also comes from the French, although it doesn't exist as a noun, but rather only as the verb "renverser" (to turn around) or as an adjective "renversé" (reversed). Its meaning is indirectly connected with the meaning of travers, which is ridden the opposite way to create the renvers, i.e. instead of the quarters to the inside, the quarters are to the outside, against the edge of the school. As a ridden exercise, in French it is called "Tête en dedans" (head to the inside) or "Croupe en dehors" (quarters out). In English the term "quarters out" is also sometimes used, which is again much more enlightening to the rider learning the movement than renvers or even counter-travers!

To keep up the structure of the book, but also to avoid burning out the reader's brain, I will keep the comparison of renvers to the other lateral movements brief.

The renvers on four tracks should only be practised in short bursts, since it demands a lot from the horse in terms of energy and concentration.

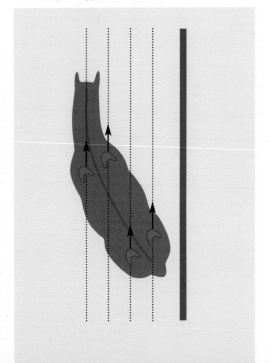

Renvers

Now that we have introduced the two main lateral movements, it is time to look at what appears to be one of the hardest – the renvers. When you consider though that the renvers is simply the mirror image of and the counter movement to the travers (which hopefully you have successfully mastered) it should not pose any problems for you. The illustration on page 75 shows that if the horse always has the same bend and angle, it is only the direction (i.e. which rein you are on) that differs – it just has another name. But it is precisely the changing direction that makes lateral movements so very interesting and valuable for the training.

When starting out and to get used to the exercise only ask for a little angle before increasing the demands and difficulty.

In addition it is not easy to keep a clear overview when, for example, if riding renvers, the bend in the direction of the movement changes so that the old inside becomes the new outside – whilst what was the outside becomes the new inside, but only so long as you don't change the rein and keep the same bend, in which case the new inside is what was the old outside and what was previously the old outside again becomes the new inside. Understood?

Renvers is the opposite exercise to travers, with the horse bent and flexed in the direction of the movement, although with renvers the forehand is brought to the inside so that now the (previous) outside fore moves beyond the (previous) inside hind. At an angle of 30 degrees the horse will move on four tracks, with the fore legs and the hind legs crossing over.

For the sake of better understanding and to maintain the horse's forwardness you should start out by asking for only a slight angle. Therefore only ask for enough to ensure that what was the outside fore moves further to the inside than what was the previous outside hind. As you become more secure in the exercise, more angle can be asked for.

Its value as a gymnastic exercise and use in training

On a straight line the gymnastic value of the exercise is little different from that of travers, except that the horse is more clearly taught to balance himself because he can't "lean" as much on to the outside of the school – as in travers — with his head, neck and shoulder. Instead these all have to move independently from the track. The positive effects on the bend through the horse's haunches, straightness, obedience to the leg, freedom through the shoulder and attention are all the same for renvers as they are with travers.

In addition there is another result of the changing from the inner to the outer bend and flexion without changing the rein. With this I create bending of the (former) outside and stretching of the (former) inside, supporting an increase in the horse's suppleness.

When training a rider, the renvers is a useful exercise to create a more effective rider in terms of the application and effectiveness of the aids.

First of all the rider and/or horse that is learning renvers should ride it in walk. It can be ridden in trot, whereby the required collection has the greatest suppling effect, so long as the horse is not too greatly angled, as otherwise the new inside hind will not take enough weight.

Aids

The aids are the same as for the travers, except that the rider has to be clear about the line being ridden and is clear that what becomes the inside of the horse is against the outside of the school. The new outside rein working together with the new inside leg brings the forehand far enough in so that anyone standing in front can clearly see the four legs, each on their own track. As there is now no wall or rail to confine the horse to what has become the outside, the outside aids have even greater significance. At the end of the exercise the rider should guide his horse back to the track using a sideways guiding rein.

Typical mistakes and corrections

As many of the mistakes made in renvers are the same as in travers, I will only add those that are specific to renvers:

By allowing the forehand too far over, the horse can escape the collecting effect of the exercise. To correct this, the rider needs to bring the forehand back over towards the outside track and re-establish the regularity of the movement.

Occasional head tilting, even for the briefest of moments, can be corrected by the rider giving slightly with the hand in the direction the horse is tilting, or through lifting the opposite hand slightly and driving through with the seat and legs. If the horse doesn't take up an even contact on both reins, then stop the exercise and start again to establish the correct flexion and bend on the circle.

It can also be helpful to change to shoulder-in for a few strides to give the muscles a rest.

It can also prove useful to simply ride into a volte from the renvers using the same bend.

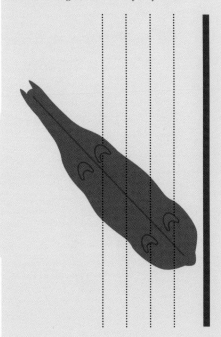

A typical mistakes in renvers: too much angle, with hardly any bend.

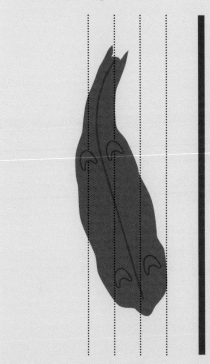

A typical mistake in renvers: too little angle, with bend only through the neck.

In order to improve the bend,
try riding a volte in the direction of the end,
before continuing with the travers.

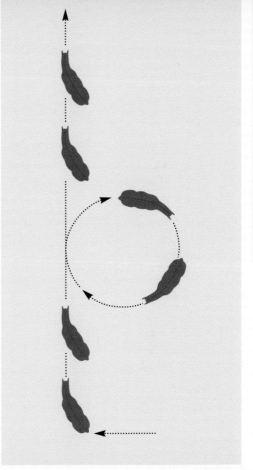

"Although shoulder-in and haunches
to the wall are excellent means for
giving horses bend, agility and a
beautiful form for where he must
go and in order to work the horse
with ease and propriety, one must
not ignore the exercises involving
trotting on straight lines and on
circles. These are the foundations
to which one must return again and
again, in order to confirm and keep
the horse's shoulders free and supple
in their movements."

François Robichon de la Guérinière

Here the renvers practised in-hand has too much angle and too little bend.

Renvers is ridden correctly when...

Here too we do not need to go into great detail since much has already been written about travers (see page 78). If you notice when riding renvers down the long side that the horse is not trying, or at least trying less, to edge back to the outside track, then you have made real progress.

Equally, if you can lengthen the stride out of the renvers without problems or without affecting the horse's balance, then this too can be seen as progress.

In summary: anything that feels smoother or easier during lateral movements is heading in the right direction.

Developing the exercise

Renvers can be introduced in a number of ways. You just have to find out which is the right way for you, and this will depend on the horse.

Here are a number of suggestions:

* Using shoulder-in the horse, whose forehand is already off the track and his hind quarters are on the track, should be re-positioned so that he is bent and flexed in the direction of the movement.

Developing renvers out of an unfinished half pass.

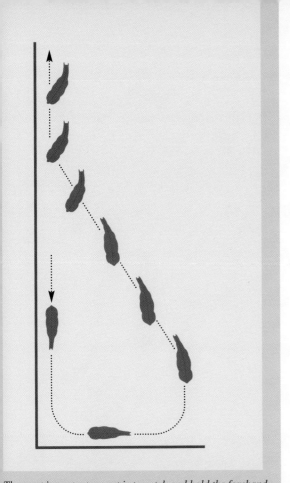

The most important aspect is to catch and hold the forehand.

Another good exercise is to ride the renvers out of a turn on the haunches.

- Using outside bend out of a corner and leading the forehand off the track you are taking up bend in the direction of the movement.
- Just before the end, a half pass: when you are about to reach the outside track, catch hold of the forehand and proceed with it on the inside track whilst the quarters swing back to the track.
- Ride a half turn on the haunches which will establish the bend required for the renvers, but before finishing it, ride the horse on parallel to outside track.
- Riding travers on a circle, change the rein out of it with changing either the flexion or bend.

The lateral movements profiled

Advanced variations

In the exercises for travers given under the same headings (see page 79) the changing from travers to renvers has already been detailed. If you now begin the same exercises in renvers and change the rein so it becomes travers, the hind leg that is closest to the track (both the former and the new) always has the job of stepping through under the horse's centre of gravity. In renvers, though, it has further to travel and so is used to work a bit more.

When changing then to travers, it keeps up its flexion but has an easier job of it because it is not travelling as far, which in turn has a positive effect on the travers. Here the principle is being followed of improving something which the horse finds difficult (in this case, travers) by asking for a greater degree of concentration and suppleness and then to return to the difficult exercise at the start.

With the help of renvers, the transition to counter canter can be prepared, for example by using the following exercise: ride a large circle at E or B, take up renvers and on the way from the centre line to E or B move into counter canter, staying on the circle for a half or even whole circle. The place where you chose to go into canter is important, since here the horse must not be turned at the same time – that would be two tasks at the same time and he may not be ready for this. Building up from this would be an exercise using the school figure described on page 76 involving leaving the track before the short side to ride a half circle against the direction you have previously moved in, changing the rein in effect back into the corner. Ride into the corner in canter but without changing leg and ride the circle in a working canter. This is especially well suited to improving the canter as it in-

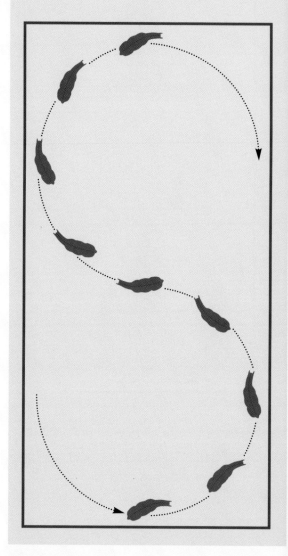

Simply change direction – renvers becomes travers.

volves a short period of collection with the inside shoulder freed.

• To prepare for the flying change, the following series of movements should prove effective: begin in walk on the circle. Then alternate between travers, canter, walk and renvers, then counter canter and again walk. Later, only hint at the walk phase before moving into canter. As you develop this

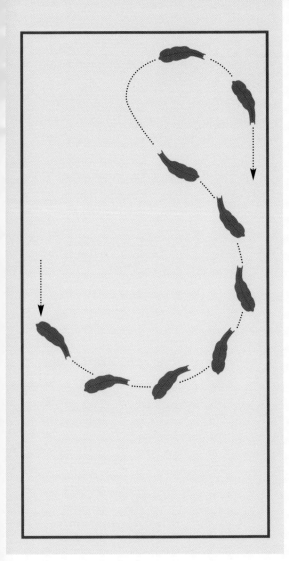

ride into the corner, riding out of it to take up half pass, from F to X, for example. Through the bend the horse is already prepared for the exercise, he just needs to know the direction to move in.

You can develop these exercises in many ways. You could use the centre line as the starting point and include lengthening and collecting. Then you can also start to think about piaffe... however you already have a lot to do with the exercises already described. And we still have to deal with the half pass – another enjoyable topic.

The half pass can be developed from renvers after the centre line.

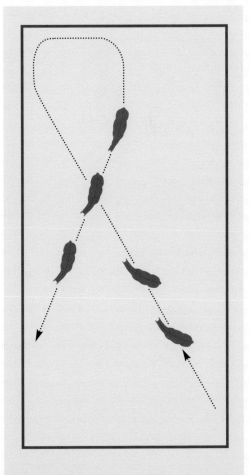

Here is another useful exercise: take up counter canter in renvers and out of the middle circle ride back into the corner.

further, give the aid for the new canter earlier and earlier. In the future then it will take less to get the horse to change leg since physically he will be well prepared and will have noticed how strenuous the transitions can be and how much easier it is to do the flying change.

- Preparation for an improvement of the half pass: refer illustration right. In renvers,

94

The half pass

Half pass

In comparison to the other lateral movements, the half pass is relatively limited in its gymnastic value. On the other hand it is a good tool to check what stage the horse's training is at. When combined with the other lateral movements you are in a position, in short bursts, to ask questions about balance, how the horse places his feet, self-carriage, seat and effectiveness of the aids. If, as a result, the horse's pace gets freer, more expressive and more collected, then the half pass was ridden successfully.

In the half pass the horse should be bent and flexed along his length in the direction of the movement. We are looking for a sideways-forwards movement along a pre-determined diagonal line, whereby the forehand to a greater or lesser degree (depending on the stage of training) leads the quarters.

The bend and degree of angle are determined by the line that is being ridden, together with the horse's ability to collect.

Its value as a gymnastic exercise and use in training

The exactness of this exercise together with the direction of the movement forwards and sideways intensifies the weight that needs to be carried on the inside hind leg, with the leg in turn carrying and pushing away this load. The outside hind is asked to cross over more. The horse's attention has more demands placed on it and the thoroughness of his training and his suppleness is being tested.

Due to the increased demands on the horse's ability to "sit" on his haunches (checking bend through the haunches and self carriage) and the forehand being lifted, we achieve more freedom through the shoulder with more elevation from the legs in the air. An observer, according to Colonel Waldemar Seunig, will see "a charming horse that impresses with his free and sublime expression".

An improvement of reaction to the aids and a different challenge for the balance can be encouraged and demanded by changes of direction – for example the zig-zag half pass. Its successful completion shows a high degree of impulsion and suppleness.

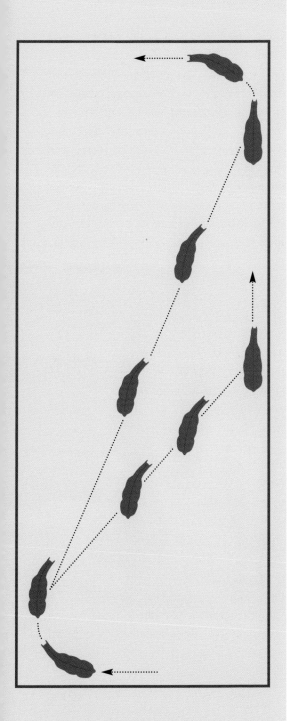

Depending on the stage of training, the half pass can be carried out on a shallow or steep angle.

Aids

Since the half pass is no different to travers on a given line, the aids are identical. In addition however – and this is the difficult part – is the forwards-sideways movement. The main influence of the rider lies in giving the diagonal aids and in the turned or rotated seat which is necessary for the sideways movement (outside shoulder and inside hip forwards).

To catch the horse's attention, and change his position and tempo, the half halt is used to get him on the aids. Using shoulder fore the horse is shown the way that is required, and the rider should only have to transfer his weight to get the horse to move sideways. Suggesting that the pupil "should think himself in front of the horse" may be helpful. The horse will then follow the rider's own centre of gravity. Once the horse is on its way, the outside leg is responsible for the sideways movement, whilst the inside leg as well as maintaining the bend and the forwardness is also responsible for encouraging the inside hind leg to lift up and step forwards.

The outside rein and the inside leg should also determine the degree of bend and the angle. The outside rein also has the job of controlling the neck at the wither, since the neck vertebrae are more mobile then the other vertebrae (see page 27) and tend rather too easily to over bend.

The inside rein looks after the flexion and the softness and controls the sideways movement. The outside leg looks after the stepping through of the hind leg on the same side as well as the longitudinal bend.

The rider ends the half pass by stopping the forehand on the inside track and for a moment riding renvers, before placing the forehand back in line with the quarters.

Developing the exercise

It is extremely important for a rider learning the half pass to grasp the idea of it being travers along a given line.

In the same way, for the horse to be familiar with travers is also very helpful, as in the following exercise: travers on the long side – half ten metre circle out of the corner – on the way back towards the track continue the bend and take the outside hind leg across.

The first half passes performed by young horses and/or by a rider who is learning the movement should only be carried out with minimum bend so that rhythm, tempo or impulsion are not lost – more in, than over!

Should you try the canter half pass, then particular attention is needed to ensure that the canter stays in balance, and remains rhythmical and uphill whilst moving sideways. This is also started with the shoulder fore. But don't be taken by surprise as it all happens very fast!

"In the case of half pass across the manège the horse, whilst maintaining his front, which it keeps in a straight line, with slight flexion and bending of the head, angled on two tracks, steps forward and sideways across the school simultaneously so that the length of his body stays parallel with the long side and a line drawn through his head and quarters falls at a right angle to the narrow end of the manège."

1825 Prussian riding regulations

"First (ride) in, then over (taking the outside legs across)."

Johann Riegler, former Oberreiter for
the Spanish Riding School in Vienna.

In the canter half pass it is particularly important to maintain the rhythmic uphill canter.

The variety of half pass movements

For the sake of thoroughness the following lists the complete variety of half pass movements. The very difficult ones are of course not immediately suitable for everyone. But it should be a case of "please look, and do try". As long as you don't overdo it, it doesn't matter if they don't work out. In show jumping you knock down jumps but still continue the course. It is obvious that the various movements should be successfully tried at some stage in whichever form they are, but it doesn't have to happen on the first attempt. Also, don't lose hope straight away, but try to find out whether you can take something positive from the attempt as it may give opportunities for corrections or further work.

The following types of half pass can be ridden: half, double half, complete, double complete as well as zig zag.

The *half travers* is the simplest example. Out of a half ten metre circle a gradual line is ridden back to the track. As training advances the line will become more exact and more will be asked.

The *simple half pass* begins on the track and extends to the centre line, although it can be done the other way around.

The *double half pass* consist of two connected half passes, usually starting from the track to the centre line at X and then back again, or starting at the centre line at A or C across to the middle marker and then back to the centre line. Think of the exercise which involves leg yielding into the school and then back out again.

Before changing direction the horse should be straightened for a length; whilst in canter half pass a flying change is completed at the change of direction.

A *(simple) complete half pass* stretches from one side of the manège to the other, on one diagonal line. This distance offers you the chance to check how well the horse maintains the crossing over of the steps, the longitudinal bend as well as rhythm and impulsion.

The *double complete half pass* by comparison comprises two complete half passes, one after the other, "there and back", across the whole of a long school (60 x 20 metres), such as K to B and B to H.

A *zig zag half pass* contains more than one change of direction, usually two, three and sometimes four along the centre line. The zig zag half pass is one of the most demanding of movements in a dressage test. Here you are asking for and testing a horse's submission, balance, responsiveness to the aids and the suppleness and forwardness on both reins.

Typical mistakes and corrections

We have already encountered most of the mistakes in the other lateral movements. For this reason I will only mention the additional ones that arise from the added forwards-sideways movement. For the sake of clarity, though, I will confine myself to the simple half pass.

Possible problems – for horse and rider	Possible causes	Solutions
In a half pass returning to the track the horse leads with his quarters (arriving before the forehand)	• The rider has paid more attention to the sideways than to the forwards	• Always remember to think of "in then over"
	• The exercise was started too early	• First go staight, then establish shoulder fore an a straight line
	• Too much bend is asked for	• Include rein aids that open the way for the sideways movement
	• The outside leg is too active	• Move into half pass right after a volte on the left rein without changing the outside leg's position
	• Rider collapses through the outside hip	• Rider needs to accentuate his own body's rotation to secure the horse's bend
	• The inside hind is overtaxed with the additional weight it is expected to bear	• Ask for less • Ride a volte to start as well as interspersing them throughout the work, possibly combined with shoulder fore
	• The suppleness sideways is lacking or is lost altogether	• Integrate voltes or figures of eight into the work
	• The horse is putting too much weight through the outside shoulder and is blocking the movement or cannot cross the outside fore over the inside	• Before the half pass (starting from the centre line) to the right, ride a volte to the left: the inside shoulder should lighten and become freer
	• The rider is asking too much, too early, and all at once, so that the aids become unclear or are even wrong	• Cut it (the problem) into pieces "Philippe Karl"
The horse won't move away from track	• The outside aids are given too early and too strongly	• Begin with shoulder fore and place more emphasis on the seat and weight aids
Horse loses rhythm	• Horse sets himself and despite this blockage (usually to the inside) rider continues to ask for the movement	• Try to loosen the blockage, don't give all the aids at once and be pleased with small improvements

Possible problems – for horse and rider	Possible causes	Solutions
The horse loses his forward impulsion	• Mental and physical demands are too great	• Ask for less sideways and more forwards movement. Then use the forwards to create the sideways
Problems with the contact, especially head tilting and moving behind the contact	• Loss of balance, too much collection being asked for when the horse is not ready for it	• Half pass in rising trot since when rising there is more focus on the forwards than the sideways • Go back to riding circles and serpentines, using this to encourage the horse through from behind into a safe contact
Too much bend through the neck	• The rider has the wrong image of what he should be asking for	• As riding instructor, come up with a new explanation • Try neck reining, i.e. riding with one hand
	• Hind quarters lack suppleness	• Go back to travers and ensure this is secure
Horse is not stepping through enough	• The horse is not being asked from behind enough • Horse is not capable of more	• Ask for more • Gradually increase the length of movement asked for
Movement goes off course	• No idea of where the exercise should be headed	• More clearly explain, show how it should be ridden or use poles to show the path that should be ridden
Horse collapses at the end, forehand drags at the end when returning to the track	• Horse lacks energy • Rider forgets that the forehand should lead	• Do the exercise again • Imagine riding mini-renvers at end

99

Think of hitchhiking. With your hand like this you will find it easier to go in the new change of direction.

The half pass is being ridden correctly when...

... the rhythm throughout the entire movement, but especially at the end, remains consistent.

... you are able to vary the tempo during and after the half pass.

... the contact remains constant.

... the horse can be asked to go straight ahead into a secure contact at any stage.

... the same amount of contact is felt through both reins.

... enough power and energy have been created so that the horse is only waiting for the chance to lengthen.

... it can be ridden in the other direction without any loss of balance.

... the angle of the half pass can be changed at any time.

... it can be ridden with one hand, or even using a neck ring.

Including voltes in the exercise gives a chance for correction when suppleness is lost or when the horse is having problems working through his quarters.

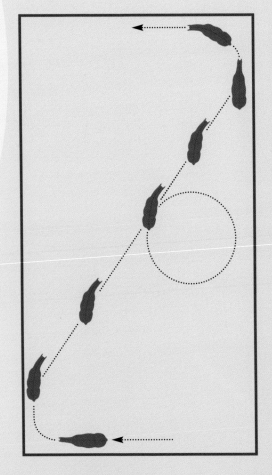 

Cantering sideways – working towards canter pirouette – using only a neck ring.

Advanced variations

Once you have established half pass as a familiar exercise, you can increase the difficulty and work on movements that the half pass helps to prepare for and improve.

In the same way as before, I am only listing a small selection, since after the initial few attempts you will undoubtedly come up with your own versions. It is important to work on improving the horse's responsiveness off the aids, balance, freedom through the shoulder, activity through the quarters and suppleness. If even the smallest of improvements is achieved then the exercise was correctly chosen. In addition if you are able to move the horse lightly off the leg and ask the horse to stretch down whenever you choose to ask, then you are heading in the right direction.

- For half pass starting away from the outside track and to benefit suppleness through the shoulder: shoulder-in down half the long side, at B or E ride a volte, then half pass to C or A.

- For a canter transition with plenty of energy, a freer shoulder in the first few canter strides as well as a clear end to the half pass: half pass in trot from the centre line back to the track after E or B, as you reach the inside track catch and hold the forehand, change the flexion to the inside and ask for canter whilst the outside hind (which was the more flexing inside hind during the half pass) still "remembers".

- To improve the precision of your riding, the suppleness of the horse's hind quarters, and your mind, for the quickly changing bend and sideways movement of the inside hind as well as the change of the balance due to the fast changes required of the exercise: from the centre line trot half pass to E or B, change to renvers back to the centre line and ride into the corner in a half ten metre circle then proceed back across the diagonal in half pass to the centre line and then ask for some lengthened strides.

For a canter transition with plenty of energy: half pass to the track and use the already active outside hind to create the first canter stride.

This exercise demands precise riding, involving half pass, renvers, changing the rein into the corner and then half pass.

As you start to development the lateral movements it is always important to ask: am I maintaining the horse's desire to move forwards ...?
Or more directly: will the horse move forward whenever I ask him to?

- To improve the suppleness of the inside hind and the ability to consciously utilise your weight to create more freedom through the shoulder on the inside: in trot, half pass from the centre line to E or B, then move into renvers on a 15 metre circle. Depending on the level of the horse and his ability to collect, after between a quarter and three quarters of the circle (which would take you back to the centre line), half pass back to the track.

As you can see, using lateral movements and mixing them with other exercises and schooling figures – even in a small way – helps to create effective and varying work. For this reason, as I said at the start, no one should be shy of trying them out. As Goethe said: "... what you don't use, is a heavy burden to carry. It is only what the moment creates, that can be used."

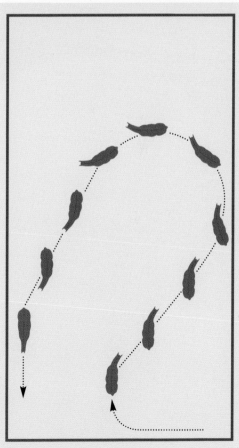

This exercise has many benefits: from half pass into renvers, then back to the centre line and half pass again.

The lateral movements profiled

Distribution of weight in the shoulder-in – a much debated question.

Shoulder-in "special"

Having covered all the lateral movements exhaustively, I would now like to return to one of my favourite topics: weight distribution in the shoulder-in.

Whilst there may be agreement in the case of nearly all the movements involved in riding regarding the seat and application of the aids, in the case of shoulder-in specifically, opinions vary widely. Its inventor, La Guérinière, expressed no particular view on how the aid should be applied. To make up for this, those following him have had plenty to say.

Less than 100 years after his death there was already a divergence of opinion. Max Freiherr von Redwitz compared various riding guidelines from 1825 until the time of writing his book about lateral work in 1900. Weight to the inside or to the outside seemed to be the main point of difference, with the opinions split evenly 50:50.

Whenever I teach I always like to carry out this live experiment: I ask my audience to shut their eyes and imagine that they were riding in shoulder-in on the right rein. Freeze this moment in time and look at yourself. Where are you placing your weight?

If you are with someone, try doing it together, as you will be surprised by the result. I have never experienced so far a group of riders, even when they have described the same distribution of weight, who have given the same justification for it.

But if it is of any comfort, the same applies even amongst the great names of riders. I have asked the same question of more than 20 trainers from differing disciplines and training methods.

It was no different to that described above. If you are watching the people in question when riding, you can hardly see any difference in the way they are distributing their weight. But their explanations for this usually have quite different thought processes.

My father, *Helmut Beck-Broichsitter,* for example, to a certain degree a proponent of the "inside", demanded this, but only in the initial stages of training. Later on, he insisted that the rider should sit in the middle so that he would be better able to match the movement.

Bent Branderup, the Danish trainer and founder of the Akademischer Ritterschaft (Academy for Classical Riding) also advocates putting the weight to the inside, on the basis that it is only then "that the horse and rider have the same centre of gravity."

"To maintain and improve impulsion whilst being uphill in his outline. To do this the horse must be in front of the rider's legs and seat." For *Christoph Hess*, head of training for the German Equestrian Federation in Warendorf, this is the most important aspect of the shoulder-in as a key movement. He would like the rider to put his weight down through his inside seat bone, whilst allowing the horse to swing through forwards and upwards.

Bettina Hoy, International eventer and amongst other successes, 2006 World Champion in the team competition, is a firm advocate of the inside aids. This applies to the riding in flexion, whether on circles or straight lines. The weight should be placed lightly on the inside seat bone to make the flexing and bending easier for the horse, and then use shoulder fore to help to create the shoulder-in. She likes to ride both on circles – not only to work on the shoulder-in but also to polish up the horse's straightness.

In the case of *Arthur Kottas-Heldenberg*, former chief head rider of the Spanish Riding School, he describes putting slightly more weight down through the inside stirrup whilst placing an equal amount of weight on both seats bones when riding shoulder-in. "There is only a hint of sitting to the right: you must always be in balance with the horse. Feeling is a prerequisite. The seat should be so secure that it is possible to ride using feeling and not strength."

One of my own trainers and former head rider *Johann Riegler* is from the same school of thought, albeit with a different starting point: he always asked for weight to the inside/back, since "only then can the horse be encouraged to flex the inside hind, step through more energetically and free up the outside shoulder at the same time".

"Outside" proponents include *Claus Penquitt*, founder of the Freizeit-Akademie (Academy for Leisure Riding), who advocates sitting to the outside in the initial training phase, so that the rider isn't sitting against the direction of the movement and possibly restricting the inside leg from crossing over. As training advances, he is agreement with Johann Riegler, albeit for reasons of encouraging the horse to step under himself more. By the end of training the rider should be sitting in the middle, since the horse should not need the aids over-emphasised by this stage.

From the outset *Richard Hinrichs* demands the same centred seat, since from this position the rider can react with a "straight vertical back" and be more effective in actively applying the aids. "In this way the horse adapts himself to the rider's movement and weight distribu-

tion", believes the head of the Institute for Classical Riding in Hanover and one of the best ever classical trainers.

"The rider can only sit in the direction of the movement when the horse is moving", is *Horst Becker's* opposing view, whereby he too recommends a centred seat. This long-time student of Freddy Knie and Kurt Albrecht however only intervenes "when there is something that needs changing".

The French Riding Master *Marc de Broissia* suggests stepping lightly into the outside stirrup to free up the inside shoulder and enable it to step through.

For *Klaus Balkenhol*, multiple German national, team world and Olympic champion, it depends on the horse stepping with his inside hind under his centre of gravity. It is only then that the hind quarters can truly step through. "In principle it should happen by itself, reacting to the lightest of aids and letting the aids through. Furthermore the rider (sitting to the inside) must first of all learn to ride straight himself. That is not that easy. If he is balanced, then you are on the way towards shoulder-in."

Christopher Bartle, who has been highly successful both riding and training in dressage and three day eventing, has his pupils apply the required weight through the inside stirrup. He describes it as if he was sharing a chair with a friend – the friend to the outside, him to the inside. But at the same time sitting up straight "as if posing for a photo".

Pierre Durand, former head of the Cadre Noir (Saumur) also advocates sitting to the inside. He succinctly describes it as follows: "In the case of shoulder-in you are trying to increase suppleness by moving a horse that is bent, sideways. The required aids are first to bend, secondly to move the curve that has been created sideways."

International show jumper *Sören von Rönne* and western rider *Peter Kreinberg* have very similar trains of thought. Both tend to ride off the track on circles or curves also using spirals (Kreinberg). If von Rönne sits more inside-back, then Kreinberg is more likely to sit quietly in the middle. His aim is more to make the aids more comprehensible to the horse.

"To the inside of the middle because of the bend," is how *Ellen Graepel*, from the Iberian equestrian world, sees the aid from the seat, since the shoulder-in is a turning in from the track that isn't however carried out. "Otherwise there is far too much theory. Riders must learn to feel."

Egon von Neindorff, former head of the eponymous Riding Institute in Karlsruhe and one of the very last great trainers of the last century, also suggests weighting to the inside but repeated to me many times that for him it was more important that the pupil developed his own feeling and empathy. Just like his horse, the rider is both a transmitter and receiver. It is the horse's feelings that should guide the rider's aids.

Phillipe Karl, former Bereiter (an honorific of someone who rides and trains horses professionally) in Saumur and now founder of the Ecole de Légèreté (School of Lightness) by comparison differentiates between the different phases of the movement. In trot on the right rein, as the left pair of legs move forwards (left fore and right hind are in the air), the rider's right hip should drop, opening up the way for greater activation of the inside hind leg. As the right pair of legs swing forward (right fore and left hind in the air) and the rider drops his left hip, this is the ideal moment to support the sideways movement by placing more weight to the left. One of his favourite questions at this stage would be, "What do you do when a child sitting on your shoulders leans to the left?"

Interestingly enough in the former East German according to the book by *Erich Oese* "Equestrianism", there was the theory that you should "distribute your weight according to the direction of the gait". This view was maintained through until the sixth, and very much reworked, edition of the book, published in 1992. From then on, "As a rule the weight should be applied on the inside (i.e. by stepping into the inside stirrup). As you start to train the horse however you should al-ways consider the principle, the rider's weight should always be applied on the side of the direction of the movement." This is according to the former president of the East German Equestrian Association.

By comparison it was a different matter in 1955 for the East German authors *Hans Huth and Bernhard von Albedyll*. "Sit to the inside in order not to interfere with the horse's freedom of movement" was the advice given in their book "The Training of Rider and Horse".

Horst Köhler, international dressage rider and multiple East German national champion in the 1960s also advocated "sitting to the inside for the sake of the horse's movement throughout the exercise".

My view of the distribution of the weight in the shoulder-in is as follows: following a circle, with weight to the inside, go large as if you are about to start the circle again at any moment. The inside leg and the outside rein are however "saying" go straight. Once the forehand has found its way off the track, you show the horse the way sideways along the track by lightly putting your weight down into the outside stirrup. "If there is nothing else to do", then the tendency is to just sit in the middle, but you must remain flexible until the end of the movement. The rider must always ensure that his aids are applied so that, just as when we build a course of cross country jumps, "he sets the horse a task that it can understand and through which it wants to do even more".

Practical
lateral work

Here I would now like to detail the riders and horses featured in this book, together with their own "problem areas". I will try to show through giving an example of a lesson, how to work through exercises incorporating the lateral movements to improve and even overcome conformation problems. We assume in every case that the horse is warmed up correctly, allowed appropriate breaks and allowed to cool down at the end. What remains is the evaluation of the actual work, "trot for the sake of trotting", as I always call it, in order to feel which changes have been worked through – taking into consideration the improvement of rhythm, regularity of the tempo, consistency of the contact and how well the horse is working through from behind.

Andrea Glink and Pico –
Making him supple with lateral work

Due to his upright hocks which caused him problems with his movement even at walk, if we introduced lateral movements to this horse too early, it would lead to him losing his rhythm – therefore definitely not something to use at the beginning of his training.

With this horse it was more a matter of making him more supple, or getting him "into gear".

Andrea Glink and Pico

111

Showing how much has been achieved: Pico takes up a good contact and is stepping through from behind.

In the trot work we included lots of work on circles and serpentines to start to hint at the lateral work thanks to the increased bend and flexion asked for on the circles, up to shoulder fore. As a step up from this we asked for rising trot but the rider rose on the wrong leg, which caused the inside hind to leave the ground more energetically (the inside hind is going to take off as the rider is sitting back into the saddle).

We don't ask for any more however, but repeatedly allow the horse forwards. The early use of canter has proved very useful for Pico. But first of all we must ensure that his transition into canter is energetic.

Since he likes to rush the standard exercises, we have developed alternatives for him. He is asked to canter out of shoulder fore on a circle, or out of counter shoulder fore in order that the outside hind leg is prepared for its job as much as possible.

Once he is warmed up and aware of what his body is doing, we can work more on his suppleness. Whilst he is more relaxed than in the earlier stages of his training, it is still hard to work him as one unit. For this reason we concentrate on specific areas, for example working on his forehand but without ignoring the haunches and vice versa. To do this we use lateral work in walk, from shoulder fore to shoulder-in on different lines. After this we include travers, but always ensuring that in between movements he is worked forwards and collected back in. To increase the difficulty, we do these exercises off the outside track and on random lines, i.e. not using the traditional schooling figures. To advance further, the same work would then be done in trot.

This shows the end result: horse and rider are on the right track.

Andrea Hinz and Cahina

Andrea Hinz and Cahina –
From impulsion to self-carriage

This mare tends to set her neck or resist by lifting her head, which makes the development of impulsion and self-carriage difficult. For this reason we work her a lot in-hand, use shoulder-in with more emphasis on the bend, travers and renvers on the circle and straight lines, as well as the counter exercises.

Again, in between movements we push her forwards so that what we have achieved in terms of suppleness sideways can be transferred to the forwards movement. To follow, to help her to swing more through her back and to maximise the "stepping through" action, under the body, from the halt we ask for the rein back with an immediate transition forwards into trot just after the last step back. From this we ask for a variation of tempo within the trot, as this reawakens the horse's desire to move forwards and maintains the suppleness that we have already achieved.

The continuation of this work then follows the usual path of rising trot and canter on both reins. After a break, we would then work on submission and self-carriage, predominantly in sitting trot, albeit in short bursts.

takes up shoulder fore for the last metre of the circle to join the track, collecting the walk for a few steps. This sequence serves to work the quarters evenly, encouraging the one then the other hind leg to greater flexion. Through the bend required on the smaller circle this will free up the shoulder and neck. To increase the difficulty of this exercise you can combine various lateral movements in quick succession.

Thanks to a clear sequence of movements and considered work a relaxed half pass causes no problems.

114   *Astrid Brinkman and Lucia*

Astrid Brinkmann and Lucia
—

Channelling enthusiasm

This mare loves her work but is sometimes rather too eager and so it is sometimes hard to channel this enthusiasm in the right direction. We have used in-hand work very effectively since this asks more of her mentally than physically. Using selected lateral movements, asking her to stretch down on a long contact and using quiet halts we have been able, over three years of work, to get her to accept the whip, ask her for the first steps of piaffe and work up to the beginnings of flying changes.

This is an extract out of the work we would do in-hand. Coming out of a volte, alternately on the right and left rein, the horse

Christina Packeiser and Lancaster

When riding, this work is continued with most attention focused on the contact and quietness in order to create and maintain Lucia's suppleness and relaxedness. The lateral movements are asked for in short bursts, partly in rising trot in order to encourage the horse to work forward but also to avoid the mare offering too much collection.

For the canter work, I ask the pair to move into an extended canter on the circle at E or B out of travers and into counter canter from renvers in order that the respective hind leg starting the canter is already prepared for the added work load as well as freeing up the inside shoulder.

From this we then develop the flying change, half pass or the beginnings of the piaffe work.

Christina Packeiser and Lancaster –
New variations on an old theme

This horse is a real "rectangular" horse covering a lot of ground, whose long legs make it easy for him to cross over his legs in the lateral work. This has a positive effect on his balance, his ability to cover ground and the development of his impulsion, but holds the danger that too much impulsion is developed at the cost of his balance and bend. What often happens with him is that he tries to find his balance by falling on to the forehand or by hurrying. He just has to see a diagonal and he takes off in a medium trot.

Since we have never had to worry about a loss of forward momentum with this horse, it proved beneficial to begin lateral work early,

By using specific exercise it is possible to achieve a canter transition with the horse waiting for the rider's aids.

at least in walk. We chose exercises that concentrated especially on freeing up his shoulders but also built on his suppleness, aiming to lift him up in front and sit him back on his haunches.

We did lots and lots of lateral work in walk when the rider felt that the forwards momentum was lost and she was needing to do too much to re-awaken him.

On the subject of medium trot: so that Lancaster didn't revert to old habits and just take off and fall on to the forehand, we started to ask for lengthening out of the shoulder-in on lines where he wouldn't normally expect to be asked. This has the advantage that we keep his attention and also that we can call on the energy that we have created through the shoulder-in in his quarters for short bursts as needed.

Another issue for this horse was a clear transition into canter. For this the counter-positions were useful, shoulder fore on the circle as well as canter and counter canter alternatively out of travers and renvers. Varying the tempo within the pace is also useful to free up the shoulder and to encourage the quarters through.

The author Johannes Beck-Broichsitter and Wallenstein.

Johannes Beck-Broichsitter and Wallenstein –

Developing trust and security using Plan C (cross country).

Before Wallenstein came to me as a six year old, so many riders had already come off him that he had a well developed fear of anything above and behind him. Interestingly though, this was only the case when he was in an environment that reminded him of dressage.

For this reason the way forward for him was obvious to me: cross country. Cantering and jumping over small obstacles in a group served initially to help him build up trust in the rider and to develop his self confidence. We did this with simple lessons that were easy for him to understand.

Running alongside this we worked on his suppleness in our indoor school – whether it was in the form of work in-hand, loose schooling over jumps, lungeing or easy suppling work under saddle. After one and half years we could then start to ride basic "dressage" flat work in the school without problems. We also started with some gentle lateral work in-hand. Now we are starting with longer periods of sitting trot, as well as more demanding cross country jumps.

Taster menu for training sessions

I would now like to offer some suggestions for structuring a lesson for both an advanced and a younger horse, based on the German Equestrian Federation's Scales of training.

First phase:
Familiarisation

The familiarisation phase in the German training tree concentrates on getting the horse used to the rider's weight and aids.

In this phase we concentrate on rhythm, freedom of movement and the contact.

- Walk on a long rein with a light contact. Think about the feeling you are getting: are either horse or rider tense? How is the horse's one-sidedness on the day? Is he concentrating and how is he feeling?
- Ride turns and circles – serpentines are a tried and tested exercise that works! By asking for lots of turns you are starting to create the idea of the horse bending around the leg. When doing this, try neck reining (rein on the horse's neck) and stepping down through the stirrup on the inside to ask for the turns.
- Start to ask for bend and straightening on both reins using kind lateral movements on the circle. Keep the reins long, so that you can still steer him where you want him but not so short that it may cause him to set himself. Start on the rein that the horse finds easier.
- Let him stretch down on the long rein in a free walk. Should the horse have problems stretching the muscles on his stiff side, try using counter bend with a shorter tempo, and then ask him to stretch again.

- Rising trot: to make the exercise both more effective and more interesting for the horse, try including a change to the balance which will also impact on the hind leg flexion by intentionally rising on the wrong leg. Change the bend regardless of which direction is being ridden on. Keep any canter work simple, but possibly think about flexion to the outside.
- Free walk on a long rein. Break and halt. Just stand for a while to give the horse a chance to relax and think.

Second phase:
Development of the forward thrust

Here you are working more on establishing a secure contact, activating the quarters and continuing the work on straightening.

- For the young horse, assuming that the beginnings of a good contact have been established, the basic paces are secure and the horse is already familiar with bending and shoulder fore: rising trot combined with canter, to wake up the forwardness; move on to work in sitting trot; using the bend and make certain he is stepping through into an even contact on both reins; assess the quality of the work; go back to rising trot and ask the horse to stretch down into a contact. This will challenge him physically and mentally.
- For the more advanced horse with straightness, balance and lateral work well established: work on suppleness by working in and out of lateral movements; always consider the forwardness of the horse. Lateral movement are only as valuable as the increase in impulsion created afterwards.

Third phase:
Development of self-carriage

Now the focus is on maintaining the impulsion, working more on straightness and turning the forward thrust into self-carriage.
- Transitions in quick succession.
- Collecting using lateral work and counter bend.
- Break.
- Build in increased difficulty with trot/halt and canter/halt transitions, lengthening and further transitions.
- Assess the quality of the work, enjoy what you have both achieved, possibly work on your seat or work with the reins in one hand.
- Walk on a long rein: are the rhythm and tempo good?
- Halt in the area you have been working in, get off and let the horse relax.

Thoughts on teaching approaches

There are a few very important points for me as a trainer that make teaching and learning so much easier and I would like to detail these briefly.
- A glance in a mirror is invaluable to assess work: does the image match the feeling. What does it look like when it feels like this?
- When an exercise is done correctly don't just say "Good" but rather ask: "Why was it like that?" How can you describe it? In this way you are helping the rider to memorise the feeling which will be a useful reference point when it is ridden again.
- The effect of a pleasant environment to ride in shouldn't be underestimated for both the

teaching and the learning process. By this I don't necessarily mean riding to the sound of a Mozart piano concerto or a Strauss waltz. But it can help greatly. Look at a pair and try to get an idea of the feeling in an environment where the radio is blasting out the news or the latest hits. It is simply less relaxed and this can prevent the horse and rider from relaxing in their work.
- Horse and rider show differences in their ability to learn. Horses are very trainable but they learn in a different way from people. They react according to what they have already experienced. Therefore the rider and the trainer must build exercises based on these experiences and approach the training process as Xenophon would have, "from easy to difficult".
- Should the horse however misunderstand the aids, we should again think of Xenophon, who warned us that "thoughtless anger, often achieves something that you will later regret". And if the same happens to the rider, then we should remember Pluvinel's words, "it is not good for the riding instructor to shout, as he is only going to scare his pupil".

Conclusion and outlook

As explained throughout this book, lateral work can be used in many different ways: from the very beginnings, working through specific exercises up to improving advanced movements. Together with other exercises they smooth the way for plan A, B or C. You cannot do without them.

One example is my now 28 year old Lipizzaner stallion Favory Roviga. He has been trained throughout his entire life and is still regularly worked. He is physically fit and virtually asks to be worked.

Precisely this attitude should be the goal of all training: to create a horse that is versatile within his capabilities. It is not important how advanced his training is. Just the fact that you are creating a harmonious picture that others enjoy watching should be enough. You can be sure that you are heading in the right direction with your training if when out hacking you can get from point A to B, ideally in canter, and the horse is always asking for more.

Anyone who has sat on a horse at least once that loved his work – whether it be medium trot, cross country jumping or a western trail course – will not want to lose this feeling and will agree with the following:

It is not difficult to teach horses.
It is harder to know when to stop.

Johannes Beck-Broichsitter

Thus lateral work is not an end in itself, but rather the means to an end — that of training a versatile horse.

Systematic training and its result.

Appendix

Acknowledgements

I would like to thank all those who played a role in creating this book.

First of all of course the riders who often were prepared to ride as I would – i.e. spontaneously: Andrea Hinz, Andrea Glink, Astrid Brinkmann and Christina Packeiser, and especially the latter, as she was also a great help in the writing of the manuscript.

To my editor Anneke Bosse who didn't have an easy job in the finalising of the text.

And of course also to the photographer Christine Slawik for the engagement she showed and the way that she always tried to take photographs from a different perspective.

My special thanks go however to my trainers and my horses, who have made me what I am today:

- To my father who provided me with a clear system of training
- To Johann Riegler, who allowed me to share in a century old tradition
- And to Philippe Karl, who by his manner and with this system gave me new direction.

My final thanks belong to my Lipizzaner stallion Favory Roviga. He spent his earliest years on the Piber stud before he started his eight years of training at the Spanish Riding School in Vienna. My family were lucky enough to be able to buy him when he was 12 years old. I did my master exams with him and from 1993 onwards travelled throughout Germany to perform and compete at almost all the Fairs and significant competitions in top hat and tails, on a loose rein, with halter or just with neck ring, performing amongst others a pas de deux with a mare.

Due to his training, talent and his toughness (two colics and three hoof abscesses in 16 years) there were never any particular areas that we had to concentrate on in his work. More than anything else, particularly when we were performing, it was a matter in the end of not being sure "Who was training whom" *(Goethe, "About Equitation")*.

In spite of his 28 years, Roviga still receives regular work. I hack him out; he is schooled to keep him supple and is used to teach carefully selected pupils the skill of working in hand or long reining.

Further reading

Advanced Techniques of Riding
German Equestrian Federation Part 2
Kenilworth Press, 2006

Behrens, Anja
Classical Schooling with the Horse in
Mind; Gentle Gymnastic training
techniques
Trafalgar Square, 2007

Behrens, Anja
In Deference
WuWei Verlag, 2006

De Kunffy, Charles
Athletic Development
of the Dressage Horse
John Wiley and Sons, 1992

Heuschmann, Gerd
Tug of War: Classical vs
Modern Dressage
J A Allen, 2007

Higgins, Gillian
How your Horse Moves: A Graphic Guide
to understanding how your horse works
David and Charles, 2009

Hinrichs, Richard
Schooling Horses In-Hand for
suppling and collecting
J A Allen & Co, 2001

Karl, Philippe
Twisted Truths of Modern Dressage
Cadmos Books, 2008

Neindorff, Egon von
The Art of Classical Horsemanship
Cadmos Books, 2009

Podhajsky, Alois
The Riding Teacher
Quiller Publications

The Principles of Riding
German Equestrian Federation Part 1
Kenilworth Press, 2006

Xenophon
The Art of Horsemanship
Dover Publications, 2006

von Ziegner, Kurd Albrecht
Elements of Dressage
Cadmos Books, 2002

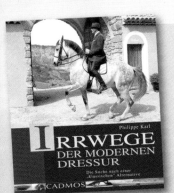

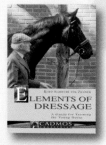